THE ALEXIS DE TOCQUEVILLE

LECTURES ON AMERICAN POLITICS

The Abolitionist Imagination

Andrew Delbanco

WITH COMMENTARIES BY
John Stauffer
Manisha Sinha
Darryl Pinckney
Wilfred M. McClay

HARVARD UNIVERSITY PRESS
Cambridge, Massachusetts
London, England
2012

Copyright © 2012 by the President and Fellows of
Harvard College

All rights reserved

Printed in the United States of America

Library of Congress Cataloging-in-Publication Data

Delbanco, Andrew, 1952–
The abolitionist imagination / Andrew Delbanco ; with
commentaries by John Stauffer, Manisha Sinha, Darryl
Pinckney, and Wilfred M. McClay.
    p.   cm.
Includes bibliographical references and index.
ISBN 978-0-674-06444-7 (alk. paper)
1. Abolitionists—United States—History—19th century.
2. Antislavery movements—United States—History—
19th century.   I. Stauffer, John, 1965–   II. Sinha,
Manisha.   III. Pinckney, Darryl.   IV. McClay,
Wilfred M.   V. Title.
E449.D45   2012
973.7'114—dc23   2011038252

CONTENTS

FOREWORD

AMERICAN ABOLITIONISM HAS EMERGED YET AGAIN AS A topic of interest in popular and academic culture, with influential studies of its individuals and its organizations. We have seen prizewinning biographies of William Lloyd Garrison, Frederick Douglass, the Grimké sisters, Gerrit Smith, and Elizabeth Cady Stanton. We have been newly introduced to the networks of black abolitionists and women abolitionists, sometimes locally centered (Boston, New York, Philadelphia, Rochester, Rhode Island), sometimes spanning state and national boundaries. And we have been reintroduced to the personal, political, and legal fruition of abolitionism with *The Fiery Trial,* Eric Foner's 2010 study of President Lincoln's confrontation with, and large-scale embrace of, abolitionist principles in the final years of his presidency and his life. Transnational historians and geographically analytic social scientists are beginning to map new pathways of abolitionist dialogue and influence across the Atlantic, within the Western Hemisphere, and within the United States. Here at the Center for American Political Studies we have joined researchers around the country in a multiyear project to catalog, digitize, and make electronically available thousands of anti-slavery petitions from the antebellum United States. And now, as the 150th anniversary of Lincoln's Emancipation Proclamation approaches, Andrew Delbanco and his respondents—John Stauffer, Manisha Sinha, Darryl Pinckney, and Wilfred McClay—reread American abolitionism anew, as a historical movement and as a persistent and dynamic metaphor in political and cultural thinking.

Delbanco's essay considers abolitionism as a general category of political vision, one impelled by "imprecatory prophets" whose contribution is, in part, to envision what their contemporaries regarded as "preposterous" and to make it seem possible. Abolitionists render a moral case against the existence and endurance of one or more of a society's perceived wrongs, such as slavery and racial castes. And perhaps others: alcohol, or gender discrimination, or abortion, or the hierarchy of heterosexuality over gay and lesbian lives. The abolitionist then and now requires moral clarity in the form of a sharp division between good and evil in which the viewer and reader can tell the two apart. Abolitionism also requires a refusal to settle for half-measures; it paints these compromises themselves as part of the problem, as resting firmly on one side of the binary divide. And, not least, abolitionism must conjure a world without the evil institution whose demise it seeks: a promised land.

Professor Delbanco's reading of abolitionism as imagination comes with a rereading of American anti-slavery itself, and its reception in the culture of the time and for a century thereafter. He seeks to understand those who, like Hawthorne or Melville, did not join the movement and who viewed abolitionists as impetuous dreamers, but who were far from defenders of slavery. He wonders, as Hawthorne and Melville did, about the limits of moral certitude in the abolitionist imagination, about the absence of concrete plans for emancipation, about the refusal to seek a middle ground. In so doing, Delbanco reminds his readers of the cultural and literary ubiquity of abolitionism in the middle and late nineteenth century.

John Stauffer sees no middle ground available for the abolitionists to have taken once the Missouri Compromise engendered a radicalism and expansionary impulse on the part of Southern slaveholders. He questions the sincerity and depth of anti-slavery convictions of Hawthorne and others, and points to the dangers of these viewpoints.

Minisha Sinha, too, finds not a square foot of centrist space to occupy in the 1830s and after. The extremism of the slave empire of the antebellum American South must not, she writes, be forgotten as the motive force in compelling abolitionists to take more rigid views and tactics themselves.

Darryl Pinckney's moving reflection offers a personal memory of abolitionism's ubiquity and reminds us of the historical consciousness of African American civil rights activists in the 1960s, who knew full well that they were acting one century after their ancestors had laid claim to freedom.

Wilfred McClay offers a different historical reading of the abolitionists, reminding us of evangelical Protestant Christianity and its internal and external conversations—with men and with God—as the primary and inescapable context of the movement. It is this cultural milieu that affords the emotive energy and driving metaphors for an abolitionist imagination.

I will not adjudicate among these judgments and contentions, or among others that emerge in the following pages. Read them for yourself, and in so doing, count yourself fortunate. The thrust and parry of argument is so persuasive that readers may find themselves drawn back and forth across the divide. Ambivalence is not customarily associated with the American abolitionists. Yet a considered ambivalence in reading the abolitionists is one of Delbanco's methods, and the debate is strong enough to induce ambivalence even if one does not, in the end, always agree with Delbanco himself.

I am struck by what these writers have together produced. By engaging in a nuanced but pointed debate about abolitionism's meaning, Delbanco and his critics achieve something they may not have intended. As the authors marshal their forces—their perspectives, historical and biographical facts, and logical and interpretive argument—a rather compact volume delivers a broad vantage. The volume becomes a reference work on American abolitionism and its meaning. It becomes a guide for understanding a vast space of action and ideas—and as any academic follower will tell you, a vast literature that takes years of reflection and reading to digest. It becomes a political, literary, historical, and cultural manual of sorts on American abolitionism, particularly the debates over the subject in the century and a half that followed it, debates that are themselves reinvigorated by this exchange.

This lecture was given as part of the Alexis de Tocqueville Lectures on American Politics, organized and sponsored by the Center for American Political Studies (CAPS) at Harvard University. Both the lecture itself and the Tocqueville series depend upon organizational and financial resources for sustenance. I wish to thank the Dean of the Faculty of Arts and Sciences, Michael D. Smith, and the deans of the Social Sciences in recent years, David Cutler, Stephen Kosslyn, and Peter Marsden. I want to acknowledge, in particular, the generosity of Terry and Betsy Considine and the Donald T. Regan Lecture Fund. I also want to thank a number of Harvard teachers and scholars whose support of the Tocqueville

Lectures has been critical to their success and who were in particular involved with this lecture: Sven Beckert, Lizabeth Cohen, Claudine Gay, Jennifer Hochschild, Harvey Mansfield, Lisa McGirr, Nancy Rosenblum, and Theda Skocpol. The Assistant Director of CAPS, Lilia Halpern-Smith, has organized every Tocqueville Lecture and continues her masterful administration of student service, community provision, and intellectual hospitality that makes CAPS what it is. Lilia is joined in her labors by the efficient and comprehensive Abigail Peck. They have my deep gratitude for work without which this event and volume would not appear as they do. Joyce Seltzer of Harvard University Press did a superb job of shepherding this book from its inception through multiple drafts to its finished form—for which I, and all the authors, are very grateful.

My final thanks go to John, Manisha, Darryl, and Wilfred, and to Andrew himself. I remember the evening fondly, and I read the exchange more fondly still, considering myself lucky to have been in the audience of this imaginative production.

DANIEL CARPENTER
Director, Center for American Political Studies
Harvard University

The Abolitionist Imagination

1

THE ABOLITIONIST
IMAGINATION

Andrew Delbanco

WHO WERE THE ABOLITIONISTS? IN REVISITING that well-worn question, my aim is not to join the long line of commentators who have drawn and redrawn the boundary between abolition proper and the broader anti-slavery sentiment of which it was a part. I want, instead, to consider the abolition movement as an instance of a recurrent American phenomenon: a determined minority sets out, in the face of long odds, to rid the world of what it regards as a patent and entrenched evil. If we construe abolition in this wider sense—in its particular manifestation in the struggle against slavery but also as a persistent impulse in American life—what might it tell us about our country?

1

One way to begin is with a quick tour of the movement from within. First of all, it is not easy to say how large it was. On the one hand, by the late 1830s, the American Anti-Slavery Society reported a membership of about a quarter-million persons in a nation of roughly seventeen million, of whom two and a half million were African American slaves. Some anti-slavery groups claimed even larger numbers of signatories on the petitions with which they lobbied Congress. On the other hand, by the outbreak of the Civil War, the subscription list of William Lloyd Garrison's newspaper *The Liberator* had dwindled to about 1,200.[1]

So this is a case where measuring by the numbers will not tell us much. What we do know is that defenders of slavery thought that abolitionists—no matter how numerous or sparse—were noxious and dangerous. In the 1830s, when an organized mail campaign flooded the slave states with pamphlets denouncing slavery, reaction "bordered on apoplexy," and as Horace Greeley later put the matter, "rulers of opinion at the South" took the view that "whoever evinced repugnance to Slavery anywhere, under any circumstances, was an Abolitionist, and an enemy of their section—a wanton aggressor upon their rights."[2]

As for the North, the distribution of antebellum attitudes looked something like this: "The population was divided into the relatively few bitter abolitionists, the large number of defenders of slavery, and the much larger number of independents not yet committed to either side of the great controversy but more and more aware of its importance."[3] So in its geographical reach, abolitionism was a national movement, at least as a goad and challenge to the standing order. It radiated out from New England through what might be called the New England diaspora—from the "burned over" districts of New York that were evangelized during the Second Great Awakening, to the Western Reserve, and, to some extent, into border states such as Missouri and Kentucky. By means of publication and rumor, it reached into the South itself, where indigenous abolitionist sentiment also existed but took the form mainly of private qualms and gestures. An elderly slave might be permitted to buy his freedom after years of saving a fraction of his wages from having been hired out; a young slave of light complexion might be freed if his master acknowledged, at least privately, that he was the slave's father.[4]

Some masters who freed their slaves may have hoped thereby to set an example that would encourage others to do the same. Almost from the first settlements, there was a good deal of hand-wringing about slavery among members of the slaveowning classes. As early as the 1730s, the patriarch of the Byrd family lamented that slaves "blow up the pride and ruin the industry of our white people, who, seeing a rank of poor creatures below them, detest work for fear it should make them look like slaves."[5] Both James Madison and Thomas Jefferson (that "ambidexter philosopher" as one abolitionist called him in the 1820s) used the word "evil" to describe slavery, although their plans for doing anything to combat the evil were invariably deferred till some indefinite future.[6] Midway between the signing of the Declaration of Independence and the adoption of the Constitution, Jefferson wrote that "the spirit of the master is abating, that of the slave rising from the dust," but he offered no timetable for when the latter would overcome the former.

In the South, hopes for an end to slavery were sometimes borne of genuine moral scruples but more often tended to reflect alarm about a growing black population—a problem for which prohibition of the African slave trade and the "diffusion" of slaves into western territories proved to be ineffective solutions.[7] Some Southern critics of slavery went further. When the North Carolinian Hinton Rowan Helper declared in 1858 that "no man can be a true patriot without first becoming an abolitionist," he, like Byrd and Jefferson before him, evinced less concern for black people than for whites. If slavery persisted, he said, the South would become a region of "niggervilles" under the rule of potentates who gave not a damn about the menial whites caught between the slaves below and the grandees above.[8] Slavery should be abolished because it was an impediment to white progress.

In short, as one historian has said with apt alliteration, the abolitionist movement was "diverse, decentralized, and divided"—so much so that it can seem a distortion to call it a movement at all.[9] Some abolitionists were concerned with the cruelties of whites toward blacks; others with the effects of slavery on whites. Some were immediatists; others were gradualists. Some regarded the Constitution as hostile to slavery; others thought the Constitution a shameful compact that must be repudiated along with the slave system, which it at least tacitly endorsed.

Some abolitionists, notably Garrison and, for a time, Frederick Douglass, considered the Union itself an obstacle to freedom and believed that all connection between free and slave states ought to be severed—an opinion widely shared before and after the secession crisis of 1860–1861, when many Northerners (not just abolitionists) were happy to see "South Carolina go, and any other states that wish to share her 'outer darkness.'"[10] Others likened the South to a rabid dog that, if cut loose, would roam "through the world poisoning nations, ruining men, women, and children yet unborn"—and therefore must be kept on a short leash till it could be brought to heel.[11]

If differences ran deep over how to analyze the problem of slavery, they ran deeper over how to attack it. Agreement on principles did not mean agreement on strategy. When John Brown confided to Douglass his intention to seize the arsenal at Harpers Ferry and to distribute its weapons to slaves, Douglass, at least by his own account, tried to persuade Brown not only that the plan would fail but that it would "rivet the fetters more firmly than ever on the limbs of the enslaved."[12] For Massachusetts senator Charles Sumner, who argued as early as 1849 for racially integrated public schools in Boston, putting an end to slavery was a step toward achieving genuine civic equality for black people.[13] Others thought the best means to end slavery was to send all blacks (including free blacks) back to their "native" Africa—a program that today we would call ethnic cleansing. Still others regarded Central America as a better place to send them and, carefully avoiding the word "abolitionist," proposed to "emancipationists of the South" that proceeds from the sale of public lands should be used to compensate them for the human property they would lose under any colonization plan.[14]

To the extent that these disputes had the character of a family quarrel, it is tempting to regard them as what Freud called "the narcissism of minor differences."[15] Especially after the Kansas-Nebraska Act of 1854 and the Dred Scott decision of 1857, when the South was regarded by many Northerners as a hostile expansionist power ("the slave power must go on in its career of exactions," said Douglass, "give, give will be its cry"), there was reason for cooperation among anti-slavery factions, whatever their differences.

So far I have been talking about abolitionists as if they were pieces on a chessboard, some more potent than others, but all predictable insofar as they could act only within the limits of their designated functions. This is, of course, a defective description. They were not instruments in the hands of some game master. Like all people, they were inconsistent and sometimes inconstant to their own professed views.

They wavered, contradicted themselves as well as each other, and repudiated ideas in which they had once believed. Douglass, for instance, who once accepted Garrison's premise that no true abolitionist should participate in electoral politics, moved to the view, in which he was encouraged by Gerrit Smith, that to "abstain from voting was to refuse to exercise a legitimate and powerful means for abolishing slavery." Sooner or later, he came to believe, government would have to be enlisted in the abolitionist cause since, as W. E. B. Du Bois was to write fifty years later, "only national force could dislodge national slavery."[16]

2

We should be wary, then, of generalizations—including, no doubt, those I have just made. This is especially true if we hope to get beyond policy positions to inner motives. For some young people, abolitionism may have been a rite of passage into adulthood; for those of blue-blood lineage, it may have been a means to mitigate their fear, in David Donald's phrase, of becoming an "elite without function."[17] For women, abolitionism may have offered a sense of efficacy in the public sphere from which they were otherwise excluded. For fugitive-slaves-turned-abolitionists, it may have assuaged what today we would call "survivor's guilt"—the feeling, that is, of having abandoned one's fellow sufferers to a fate one has escaped. Some abolitionists were merciless toward slaveowners; others saw themselves as Good Samaritans rescuing not only slaves from masters but masters from themselves—since, again in Du Bois's words, "the degradation of men costs something both to the degraded and those who degrade."[18]

Never a unified party, abolitionism was in some respects radical, in others conservative. While participation in the cause may have furnished a variety of psychological rewards—both conscious and unconscious—there is no reason to question the passion and sincerity of those who enlisted in it. It was a movement that looked forward to a world reconstructed on a new principle of universal liberty, but it also looked backward to Jefferson's neoclassical ideal of "temperate liberty," the sine qua non of republican citizenship—which, it said, the slavery regime undermined for slave and slavemaster alike. "The slave is a subject, subjected by others," as Douglass put it, but the "slaveholder is a subject" as well—"the author of his own subjection." This was Douglass the transcendentalist ("every new-born white babe comes armed from the Eternal presence, to make war on slavery"), who sees each person as a moral being *in potentia*— distorted and deranged by a system that imprisons the soul and consigns both slave and slaveowner to a "little nation of [his] own," where "appetite, not food, is the great *desideratum*."[19] Abolitionists belonged self-consciously to the tradition of imprecatory prophets; they were the thundering Isaiahs and Jeremiahs of their time, calling to account this fallen world and exploiting the fear of apocalypse if they should fail.

Accordingly, Douglass included in his autobiography scenes of violence that seem to say, Look at me, gentle reader: if you hope to save yourselves, you must first save me. Men like me—angry black men, cut off from the softening influences of family and friends, confined to the sordid "*present and the past*"—are longing for "a future—a future with hope in it." If you deny us this hope, we will become monsters.[20] Slavery is the factory of the South, and what it is producing—indeed, mass-producing—is black rage.

The shadings I have just sketched were generally absent from the picture of abolitionism as seen through the eyes of unsympathetic contemporaries, which is to say, most contemporaries. To their enemies, abolitionists seemed to be fanatics pure and simple. They wanted the world purged of slavery, and, by and large, they wanted the purging to start now. "I do not wish to think, or speak, or write, with moderation," as Garrison announced in the inaugural issue of *The Liberator*. "No! no! Tell a man whose house is on fire to give a moderate alarm; tell him to moderately rescue his wife from the hands of the ravisher; tell the mother to gradually extricate her babe from the fire . . . but urge me not to use moderation in a cause like the present. I am in earnest—I will not equivocate—I will not excuse—I will not retreat a single inch—and I WILL BE HEARD."[21]

This kind of talk was received in the South as the rant of an "unHoly crusade" threatening the very foundations of society. If not checked, it would force even the kindest slavemasters to draw the sword "against our own property," whose putatively childlike minds were being excited by fantasies of freedom. Slaveowners who dismissed abolitionists as dreamers and fools nevertheless took seriously the abolitionist portrayal of slaves as restive and potentially rebellious, even as they remained convinced—or at least tried to persuade themselves—that any discontent among their slaves was incited rather than intrinsic to their condition. "Strange that they should be alarmed," as Harriet Jacobs wrote in her remarkable memoir, *Incidents in the Life of a Slave Girl* (1861), "when their slaves were so 'contented and happy'! But so it was."[22]

On both sides of the regional divide, to call someone an abolitionist was to denounce or deride him. What abolitionists took up as an honorable name was in fact a name assigned to them as a term of opprobrium. The very word "abolitionism" (in this respect, it was like the word for an earlier reform movement, Puritanism, to which not a few leading abolitionists could trace their ancestry) was usually uttered as a slander meant to convey what many Americans considered its essential qualities: unreason, impatience, implacability. When Stephen Douglas, the last major politician to give up the idea of a bisectional political party, wished to mock his opponent in the Illinois senatorial campaign of 1858, Douglas likened him to "the little abolitionist orators in the church and school basements."[23] It was Douglas's way of trying to make his tall opponent seem small. Two years later, when that opponent, Abraham Lincoln, went to New York to audition before the kingmakers of the Republican Party, he had to make sure the abolitionist label had not stuck. To that end, he distanced himself from the most notorious of all abolitionists, John Brown, in much the way that, 150 years later, presidential candidate Barack Obama felt compelled to distance himself from Jeremiah Wright and Bill Ayers.[24]

3

Almost everything I have said so far concerns the abolitionists before the outbreak of the Civil War. The war, of course, changed everything—and as with every war, its consequences were unforeseen and largely unintended. Both sides went into it in a swoon of insouciance—the mood in which so many wars begin. (Who can forget Secretary of Defense Donald Rumsfeld's promise at the start of the Iraq war that first would come "shock and awe," then plaudits and laurels for the liberating army?) No one, as Lincoln said after four years of fire and blood, expected a conflict of such "magnitude or duration." Southerners underestimated Union sentiment in the North so badly that one Southern senator vowed to drink all the blood that would be shed as a result of secession. If there was to be a war, it would be quick—a sort of ceremonial duel, to be followed by toasts and handshakes and maybe a cotillion ball.

Northerners underestimated southern resistance just as badly. When the "monster Act" (Sumner's phrase for the Fugitive Slave Law of 1850) was compounded four years later by the Kansas-Nebraska Act, the abolitionist Richard Hildreth ridiculed "the prophecies of our southern friends" that "the struggle that impends" will "shake the country to the centre" and "end . . . in infuriated hostilities and savage war."[25] In this respect, at least, they were right and he was wrong. In a series of poems written toward the end of the war, Herman Melville recalled local Massachusetts boys "marching lustily / Unto the wars, / With fifes, and flags, in mottoed pageantry," never dreaming "that Death in a rosy clime / Would come to thin their shining throng."[26] But thin them it did—by more than half a million, counting the losses on both sides. As the "great convulsion" (Henry James's retrospective phrase) dragged on, it brought death on an unprecedented scale—not only by shot and blade but by gangrene, dysentery, and starvation, leaving a generation to die in the dust and mud and, for the survivors, leaving everything changed.

Among the changes were prospects for the abolitionist cause. At the outset of the war, one of President Lincoln's advisers told the Republican governor of Massachusetts to "drop the nigger" when it seemed the governor was thinking of telling the state legislature that the war had something to do with liberating slaves.[27] Pro-Union newspapers insisted that the war had nothing to do with slavery except in the limited sense of keeping it out of the federal territories.

But two years into the fighting, the editor of one such paper, Horace Greeley of the *New York Tribune,* chided Lincoln for moving too slowly against slavery in the slave states themselves. The anti-slavery clergyman William Greenleaf Eliot, who had moved from Massachusetts to Missouri, a slave state that remained loyal to the Union, wrote that "the war, or rebellion (as you may be pleased to call it) begun for the defense and support of Slavery, has done more for its restriction and partial removal, and probably for its early overthrow, than all the friends of Emancipation combined could have done, by whatever means."[28]

Of course it did not happen at once. In the first phase of the war, with things going badly for the North, and with a peace party forming on the platform of restoring the status quo ante, abolitionists looked to many people on both sides of the conflict like warmongers on behalf of an unwinnable cause. But as the fortunes of the Union improved, in order to spare their troops from the burden of managing human "contrabands," as well as to deprive the enemy of its coerced labor force, officers in the field began to act on their own authority to free slaves who came under their control. At first, it was more a matter of military strategy than of moral principle by which the "Secession War," as Walt Whitman called it, came to be reconceived, in the words of Thomas Wentworth Higginson, as a "war for freedom."[29]

The most important convert to the new view was Lincoln himself, who had begun his presidency by assuring the South, to the disgust of abolitionists (Wendell Phillips called him a "huckster" and "slave hound"), that he had no intention to interfere with slavery where it existed.[30] By the summer of 1862, however, his mind was opening to new possibilities. In August, he wrote to Greeley that "my paramount object in this struggle is to save the Union," and "if I could save the Union without freeing any slave I would do it, and if I could save it by freeing *all* the slaves I would do it, and if I could save it by freeing some and leaving others alone, I would also do that."

This statement is sometimes construed—wrongly, in my view—as an expression of Lincoln's indifference to the fate of the slaves. In fact, it registered his growing recognition that the war would be the instrument of liberation that abolitionists had been urging him to wield. When he wrote to Greeley, it is likely that, needing the loyalty of the slaveholding border states, he had already made up his mind to exercise the third of the three options—"freeing some and leaving others alone." A month later, when he issued the preliminary Emancipation Proclamation warning secessionists that on the first day of the coming year all slaves would be freed in states that had not laid down their arms against the national government, he knew that a voluntary cease-fire was not about to happen. Eleven months after that, at the dedication of the vast Union cemetery at Gettysburg, Lincoln finally became an avowed abolitionist in the sense that, for the first time in public, he construed the war as having granted the nation a "new birth of freedom"—a phrase he left unelaborated but that implied the convergence of his public policy with what he had called, in the letter to Greeley, "my oft-expressed *personal* wish that all men every where could be free."[31]

In that summer of 1862, as it became clear that the manpower demands of the Union army exceeded the supply that could be provided by enlistment or conscription, Lincoln approved the arming of black volunteers. By late 1863 he was telling the nation that his "policy of emancipation, and of employing black soldiers" had given "to the future a new aspect." Against those who had predicted otherwise, he noted that "no servile insurrection, or tendency to violence or cruelty, has marked the measures of emancipation and arming the blacks." And, in an extraordinary expression of both humility and pride, he thanked *all* the soldiers, black and white, to whom "the world must stand indebted for the home of freedom disenthralled, regenerated, enlarged, and perpetuated."[32] Lincoln, who had struggled to reconcile the universal equality principle of the Declaration of Independence with the recognition of slavery implicit in the Constitution, was coming around to Sumner's view that "the word 'person' in the Constitution embraces every human being within its sphere, whether Caucasian, Indian, or African, from the President to the slave."[33]

Perhaps the most authoritative witness to Lincoln's development was the former slave Frederick Douglass. A decade after the president's assassination, Douglass said of him that "viewed from the genuine abolition ground," he may have "seemed tardy, cold, dull, and indifferent," but, in retrospect, his

great mission [had been] to accomplish two things: first, to save his country from dismemberment and ruin; and, second, to free his country from the great crime of slavery. To do one or the other, or both, he must have the earnest sympathy and the powerful cooperation of his loyal fellow-countrymen. Without this primary and essential condition to success his efforts must have been vain and utterly fruitless. Had he put the abolition of slavery before the salvation of the Union, he would have inevitably driven from him a powerful class of the American people and rendered resistance to rebellion impossible.

This was a repudiation of the view, held by many abolitionists, that Lincoln had been a malingerer. Douglass disagreed: "Measuring him by the sentiment of his country, a sentiment he was bound as a statesman to consult, he was swift, zealous, radical, and determined."[34]

4

But family differences, muted or suppressed in the face of a common threat, have a way of coming back once the threat has passed. After Appomattox, some surviving elders of the movement interpreted the war as a we-told-you-so vindication of their cause against those who opposed or retarded it, including Lincoln. They presented the history of abolitionism as that of a persecuted church, complete with prophets (William Ellery Channing), martyrs (Elijah Lovejoy, John Brown), and apostles (themselves) who survived to give testimony of the miraculous fulfillment of the original faith. Years after the war, Higginson was still berating Lincoln for his putative vacillation, for "defending liberty with one hand" while "crushing it with the other," while Douglass—and no one had been hotter for the cause—saw Lincoln as liberty's champion and martyr.[35]

By the mid-1870s, with the campaign to extend citizenship rights to emancipated slaves foundering in the South, we find abolitionists reliving old quarrels. The old abolitionist George W. Curtis railed against the old abolitionist Charles Sumner for having supported the presidential candidacy of the old abolitionist Horace Greeley. It was, said Curtis, the saddest moment in American politics since Daniel Webster endorsed the Fugitive Slave Law.[36] And if they resumed debating with each other, they sometimes dissented retrospectively from their former selves. Higginson, one of the "secret six" who had financed John Brown, reflected on the once-heated arguments over whether black men would make reliable fighters in the Union cause. Moved by the courage of black soldiers under fire, he came to the conclusion that "we abolitionists had underrated the suffering produced by slavery among the negroes, but had overrated the demoralization."[37]

This kind of postwar revaluation took place, of course, in an utterly changed context of judgment. If before the war abolition had been denounced as a form of "monomania," after the war, more and more Americans—on the principle that everyone loves a winner—claimed to have been abolitionists all along. Every farmhouse had been a station on the Underground Railroad; everyone's father or grandfather had been a conductor; every home had had a secret pantry where Sambo had been fed and clothed or an attic where Sally had been hidden when the bounty hunters came pounding on the door. Embracing abolition retrospectively became a way to lay claim to what David Blight has called an "alternative veteranhood," a way to satisfy the "yearning to bask in the glory of the old abolitionist generation."[38]

As the struggle against slavery passed from personal memory into the hands of historians, the contest over the meaning of abolitionism entered yet another phase. The first extended assessments came from historians who had lived through the conflict. George Bancroft, a lifelong Democrat who had reached age sixty by the outbreak of the Civil War, had been wary of abolitionists but eventually came to see them as God's instruments in banishing slavery from the New World. The more secular-minded James Ford Rhodes, who was only in his teens during the war and did not turn to writing history till the 1890s, credited "organized antislavery agitation" (his synonym for abolitionism) with having shifted British public opinion from the Confederacy to the Union, especially once Lincoln adopted abolition as the policy of his government and thereby turned "those Englishmen who had espoused the cause of the South" into shameless "apologists for slavery."[39]

But even in the victorious North, the postwar rehabilitation of abolitionism was far from universal. As late as 1913, we find John Jay Chapman, whose circle encompassed Boston and New York, reporting that a "learned friend," upon hearing that Chapman had written a favorable biography of Garrison, burst out, "A book about William Lloyd Garrison? Heave a brick at him, for me!"[40] In the same year, President Woodrow Wilson gave an address marking the fiftieth anniversary of the battle of Gettysburg that amounted, as Blight has pointed out, to a kind of neo-confederate erasure of slavery from public understanding of what was at stake in the Civil War. Wilson, an academic historian himself, spoke of battlefield valor and sectional reconciliation but said barely a word about slavery or those who opposed it.

Published five years later, Ulrich B. Phillips's *American Negro Slavery,* a book that became for a generation the dominant interpretation of the antebellum South, portrayed the peculiar institution as a form of benevolent paternalism. As for historians' treatment of the abolitionist legacy—notably the effort to enfranchise former slaves after the war— William Dunning's hugely influential *Reconstruction: Political and Economic, 1865–1877* (1907) adopted the anti-abolitionist view of blacks as uncivilized creatures incapable of self-government, and within a few years, D. W. Griffith's film *Birth of a Nation* (1915) had established this view as a popular norm.

Ever since, the fortunes of the abolitionists, in both popular and academic accounts, have continued to wax and wane. Writers of Marxist bent have portrayed them as instruments of Northern money interests—promoters, as one historian puts it, of "a theory of capitalist morality" in the form of the free labor ideology. This view echoes antebellum critics of antebellum Northern factory culture, such as one aggrieved plantation mistress who complained that Union troops aimed to dupe "Africa's poor sons and daughters, to lure them on to ruin and death of soul and body" in the North as cheap, and reliably supine, laborers.[41] Before the war, pro-slavery apologists such as the South Carolinian James Henry Hammond had assailed Northerners with the charge that the "whole hireling class of manual laborers and 'operatives,' as you call them, are essentially slaves"—a critique of Northern industrialism that would eventually find its apotheosis, without any taint of apologetics for slavery, in the work of the historian Eugene Genovese. On such a view, abolitionists look more like accomplices in the work of subjugation than agents of liberation.

5

By the late 1940s and into the 1950s, abolitionists were coming under a different kind of critique—this time not from the political right or left but from the center. The antebellum Republican policy of holding the line against the expansion of slavery now seemed a laudable preview of the Cold War policy of "containment" in a world over which two incompatible social and economic systems were struggling for mastery.

In this perspective, Lincoln became an advocate of realpolitik who understood the limits of power and the perils of intervention—a kind of forebear of Dean Acheson and George Kennan. With patience and stamina, Lincoln seemed to have believed, containment would eventually lead to the death of the rival system. In his firmness without belligerence, he exemplified the kind of leadership required in times of crisis. In such books as Roy Franklin Nichols's *The Disruption of American Democracy* (1948) (dedicated to Dunning), those who urged concessions to the slave South were fellow travelers or appeasers, while those who agitated for intervention were reckless fools. The best way was the middle way.

By the 1960s, the pendulum was swinging back toward the abolitionists and away from Lincoln, who now came under attack not just as a footdragger on slavery but as a white supremacist.[42] Historians began to pay attention again to divisions within the abolitionist ranks—between blacks and whites who sometimes collaborated but at other times fell into dissension; between those who called for armed slave revolt and those who counseled nonviolence; between integrationists who envisioned a biracial society and separatists who believed that only in a nation of their own could emancipated slaves attain real dignity.[43] The antebellum campaign for black voting rights and for desegregating public conveyances such as New York City's streetcars seemed to anticipate the civil rights struggles of more recent times, as did the debate within the movement over whether abolitionists should make alliance with advocates of women's rights. Abolitionism had now become a mirror of post-1960s America.[44]

Reflected in that mirror was one group that had hitherto been largely invisible: white Southern women, who, according to the mistress of one Georgia plantation, were "all at heart abolitionists," and who—perhaps out of sympathy, perhaps out of jealousy—recoiled, at least privately, from the sexual exploitation of female slaves by their own husbands. Another hitherto overlooked group—arguably the most important in the anti-slavery alliance—now came into view: the slaves themselves. We have yet to achieve a full understanding of their role in the work of emancipation, but thanks to such scholars as Ira Berlin, Barbara Fields, and Manisha Sinha, we are getting closer. Using new digital technologies that allow the detailed correlation of troop movements with the movements of former slaves, historians are also beginning to map what Gary Gallagher, in his recent book *The Union War* (2011), calls "the geography of emancipation"—with the aim of obtaining a better sense of how, as Union forces advanced, slaves took advantage of opportunities to liberate themselves.[45]

As for the role of abolitionists in politics more traditionally understood, we seem today to have arrived at what I would call, with due deference to my Columbia colleague, the Foner synthesis. In *The Fiery Trial: Abraham Lincoln and American Slavery* (2010), arguably the best account yet written of Lincoln's thinking about slavery, Eric Foner presents abolitionists neither as canny strategists within the Republican coalition nor as a radical fringe group outside the party. In his telling, they were passionate idealists who enlarged the imagination of mainstream politicians—above all, Lincoln himself—by awakening "the nation to the moral imperative of confronting the problem of slavery."

Invoking Max Weber's great essay "Politics as a Vocation" (1918), Foner gives us a Lincoln who met all of Weber's criteria for effective politics: commitment to a cause, a sense of responsibility, and awareness of the consequences of political action. But he also reminds us, via Weber, of the changeable context in which politics as the "art of the possible" must be carried on: "What is possible would not have been achieved, if, in this world, people had not repeatedly reached for the impossible."[46] For Foner, the contribution of the abolitionists was to make thinkable what had once been unthinkable, namely, black freedom. By pushing beyond conventional ideas about race and slavery, they changed both Lincoln's private judgment and public opinion, thereby vastly enlarging what was politically possible in nineteenth-century America.

I hope by now I have said enough to suggest that every generation has offered a different answer to my opening question—"who were the abolitionists?" The history of historiography reminds us that, in due course, every consensus splinters or shifts, and there is no reason to doubt that this process of continual revision will continue. Nearly a century and a half has now passed since, with the adoption of the Thirteenth Amendment, the abolitionists achieved the goal of terminating slavery as a legal institution—and we seem to have arrived at what one historian calls retrospective "consecration" of their cause.[47] Yet the question remains: what is at stake in how we understand them?

6

Any serious answer, to borrow the well-known phrase from William Faulkner that then-Senator Obama used in his remarkable speech on race during his 2008 campaign for the presidency, must begin with the recognition that "the past is not dead. In fact, it is not even past." On that view, abolition may be regarded not as a passing episode but as a movement that crystallized—or, as we might say today, channeled—an energy that has been at work in our culture since the beginning and is likely to express itself again in variant forms in the future. If, in fact, there is such a current in American life, surely we should want to know why it is sometimes active and sometimes dormant, and why—improbable as it seems to us today—some people of good will and liberal sentiments have resisted it. To ask these sorts of questions is, I think, to broaden our inquiry beyond the kind of documentary texts on which I have so far relied and to include works generally assigned to the category of literature. It is to construe abolitionism not only as a historically specific movement but as an ahistorical category of human will and sentiment—of what we might even dare to call human nature. It is to suggest that we have not seen the last of it, and probably never will.

In this broader view, an abolitionist is not a member of this or that party but is someone who identifies a heinous evil and wants to eradicate it—not tomorrow, not next year, but now. Prince Hamlet of Denmark, who sees "time . . . out of joint" and believes himself "born to set it right" is an abolitionist—albeit a reluctant one. Don Quixote, who tells Sancho Panza that he was "born in this age of iron" with a duty to restore "the age of gold," is an abolitionist. Kirilov in Dostoevsky's novel *The Possessed* (also translated as *The Devils*), who is prepared to commit suicide to usher in the millennium, is an abolitionist. Indeed every millenarian dreamer who has ever longed for the fire in which sin and sinners are consumed is an abolitionist—and sometimes the purification will include his own self-immolation.

To open the question in this way is, of course, to open it to a vast array of commentators over many centuries and cultures. In order to keep things manageable, I will limit myself to two authors who witnessed the emergence of abolitionism in its specific American form. These two authors— Nathaniel Hawthorne and Herman Melville—were astute witnesses to their times, but they also understood abolitionism as a transnational and transhistorical phenomenon.

Given his tendency to stay aloof from the political contentions of his day and to set his fictional tales in the picturesque past, Hawthorne may seem an odd first choice. But abolitionists were on his mind early on. Sometime around 1835 (the entry has not been precisely dated), he jotted in his journal an idea for a story:

> A sketch to be given of a modern reformer,—a type of the extreme doctrine on the subject of slaves, cold water, and other such topics. He goes about the streets haranguing most eloquently, and is on the point of making many converts, when his labors are suddenly interrupted by the appearance of the keeper of a madhouse, whence he has escaped. Much may be made of this idea.[48]

To us, it will be startling to find a medical fad—the cold-water cure, otherwise known as hydrotherapy—lumped together with the "extreme doctrine on the subject of slavery" as a weird and pointless fixation. For most of Hawthorne's readers, however, the linkage was perfectly natural. To the extent that no one in antebellum America had a plausible plan for ending slavery, "abolitionist" was a synonym for dreamer.

A few years after that notebook entry, Hawthorne followed up his own suggestion. In a minor sketch called "The

Hall of Fantasy" (1843), he offered a fanciful picture of "a spacious hall, with a pavement of white marble," a "public Exchange" where crackpot inventors gather to hawk their wares. The devices on display include "a machine . . . for the distillation of heat from moonshine" and another "for the condensation of morning-mist into square blocks of granite." Among the exhibitors is "the abolitionist, brandishing his one idea like an iron flail"—as monomaniacal in his way as the slaveowner with whip in hand, whom Hawthorne evoked with the image of the brandished flail.[49]

Yet despite this suggestion of symmetry between the enemies and friends of slavery, Hawthorne writes about abolitionism in a spirit that is by no means dismissive. He is almost envious ("it was good for the man of unquickened heart to listen even to their folly") in admitting that his own temperament does not allow for dreaming. "My faith revived," he writes in the voice of his narrator, "even while I rejected all their schemes."[50] Dreamers exert on him a simultaneous attraction and repulsion. This state of in-betweenness was a place to which he was drawn in his best work as well as his hack work—as, for instance, in the puff biography he wrote in 1852 for the presidential campaign of his Bowdoin College classmate Franklin Pierce. Sometimes cited as evidence of Hawthorne's putative Copperhead sympathies, even that thin book contains hints of ambivalence on the slavery question—as in the portrait of one candidate for the governorship of New Hampshire, John Atwood, who destroyed his political career by oscillating between saying yes and saying no to the Fugitive Slave Law. Having "attempted first to throw himself upon one side of the gulf, then on the other," he "tumbled headlong into the bottomless depth between."[51]

At the edge of this abyss is where we find many of Hawthorne's fictional protagonists and where, I think, Hawthorne frequently found himself. "His mind," as one contemporary put it, was "always hovering between two views."[52] Consider the early story "My Kinsman, Major Molineux" (1831), in which he explores the divided consciousness of a young man who finds himself in a sort of Walpurgis Night of mingled horror and pleasure, swept up by the spectacle of a torch-bearing mob that seems to invite him to join their blood orgy as they parade a tarred-and-feathered member of the ruling caste through the streets. Simultaneously excited and repelled, the young man wants to join, but he also wants to flee, especially when it turns out that the victim of the mob is the very "kinsman" whom he has been seeking.

Or consider Hawthorne's masterwork, *The Scarlet Letter* (1850), in which the fire-eyed Hester Prynne, a beautiful young woman locked in loveless marriage to a desiccated old man, leads her young lover into the forest, unclasps her raven hair, and, infecting him with her antinomian spirit, carries him—a sober and settled minister—to the edge of a radically new life consecrated to their adulterous passion. The writing is so charged that one suspects the author of giving vent to his own yearnings:

> There played around her mouth, and beamed out of her eyes, a radiant and tender smile, that seemed gushing from the very heart of womanhood. A crimson flush was glowing on her cheek, that had been long so pale. Her sex, her youth, and the whole richness of her beauty, came back from what men call the irrevocable past, and clustered themselves, with her maiden hope, and a happiness before unknown, within the magic circle of this hour.[53]

But Hawthorne pulls back from his own ravishing symbol. He returns the lovers—she as mother, he as minister—to their social responsibilities. After her lover's death following an act of public penitence, and after her long self-imposed exile with their now-fatherless child, Hester returns to the scene of her youthful passion as a counselor to young women. She tries to help them come to terms with their own sense of confinement by assuring "them, as best she might . . . of her firm belief, that, at some brighter period . . . when the world should have grown ripe for it, in Heaven's own time, a new truth would be revealed in order to establish the whole relation between man and woman on a surer ground of mutual happiness." She has not relinquished her hope, but she has deferred it.

The Scarlet Letter is filled with seventeenth-century locutions such as "thee" and "thine," yet its idiom was unmistakably that of the contemporary women's movement, to which Hawthorne was connected through his circle, including the Alcotts, Peabodys (his wife's family), and Margaret Fuller, editor of *The Dial* and author of *Woman in the Nineteenth Century* (1845), who had been, in the summer of 1842, his Concord neighbor.[54] And he knew that the feminists of his day were increasingly engaged, or at least allied, with the anti-slavery movement. For the portrait of Hester as well as of the magnetic Zenobia in *The Blithedale Romance* (1852), he likely had Fuller in mind, who, as correspondent for Greeley's *Tribune* in Italy during the revolutionary 1840s, embraced the cause of abolition as inseparable from the cause of women's—and, more broadly, human—rights.

Sympathetic to the abolitionists' "aims," Fuller demurred at their "measures," until, swept up in the rising excitement of Italian nationalism, she came close to countenancing assassination as a political tactic. It is not fanciful to imagine

Abolitionist as well as Adulteress and Anarchist among the "A-words" Hawthorne had in mind when he placed the scarlet letter on Hester's breast. After her public humiliation, he recalls her from radicalism to reason—or, to use the prevailing terms of the day, from immediatism to gradualism. "Earlier in life," we learn near the end of the novel, Hester "had vainly imagined that she herself might be the destined prophetess, but had long since recognized" that the jubilee day of freedom must be postponed till some indefinite future.[55]

This dividedness over the value and cost of freedom is a persistent theme in Hawthorne's writing from the early stories to his late works, including in his most direct reflection on the Civil War, an article entitled "Chiefly about War Matters" published pseudonymously in 1862 in the *Atlantic* under the name "A Peaceable Man." In that essay, he describes a group of fugitive slaves trudging north from the war zone and allows himself a frank reflection that is often cited as evidence of his lukewarmness to the cause of emancipation:

> For the sake of the manhood which is latent in them, I would not have turned them back; but I should have felt almost as reluctant, on their own account, to hasten them forward to the stranger's land; and I think my prevalent idea was, that, whoever may be benefited by the results of this war, it will not be the present generation of negroes, the childhood of whose race is now gone forever, and who must henceforth fight a hard battle with the world on very unequal terms.[56]

In fact, this was an example of Hawthorne doing what he always did: arguing with himself. As F. O. Matthiessen put the matter, "the characteristic Hawthorne twist" was his habit, after making any decisive assertion (as when he called slavery "one of those evils which divine Providence does not leave to be remedied by human contrivances, but which, in its own good time . . . [will] vanish like a dream")—"to perceive the validity of its opposite."[57] And so, in the *Atlantic* article, he not only acceded to the editors' insistence that the essay could be published only if accompanied by dissenting footnotes, but he supplied the annotations himself. "The author seems to imagine," he wrote in one note, that he has "compressed a great deal of meaning into" his "little, hard, dry pellets of aphoristic wisdom. We disagree with him." What we have here is a politically unclassifiable writer—a damning fact, perhaps, to those who believe that neutrality, indifference, and collusion are names for the same shameful thing and that, regardless of the claims of ambiguity upon the literary imagination, there are times when a writer must choose sides.

7

The topics that kept Hawthorne and his Berkshire neighbor Herman Melville talking late into the night when they first became friends in the summer of 1850 very likely included reform and reformers. Both men were connected to key figures involved in the dispute over the Fugitive Slave Law that broke out that spring and summer in Boston. Hawthorne had belonged to the Concord circle in which abolitionist sentiment was strong. In the spring of 1851, despite his doubts about abolitionist action, he signed a petition protesting the Fugitive Slave Law, while Melville's father-in-law, Chief Justice Lemuel Shaw of the Massachusetts Supreme Judicial Court, stood at the center of the firestorm as a reluctant defender of the law. Unfortunately, we will never know what they said privately to one another about this or other public issues of the day.

What we do know is that in turning from Hawthorne to Melville, we turn from a writer who could be coy and oblique—*The House of the Seven Gables* [1852], a book in which slavery is never mentioned, begins with the observation that "the wrong-doing of one generation lives into the successive ones, and, divesting itself of every temporary advantage, becomes a pure and uncontrollable mischief"—to a writer who, by comparison, was overwrought and blunt. Hawthorne's disapproval of slavery was always more regretful than incensed. Melville denounced it as a "sin . . . no less;—a blot, foul as the crater-pool of hell." Hawthorne knew hardly any black people by direct acquaintance. Melville, having spent a good part of his youth aboard whaleships and warships, had experienced the closest thing in antebellum America to a racially integrated society. "Humanity cries out against this vast enormity," he said of slavery. And yet his sense of the political impasse over what to do about it was at least as acute as Hawthorne's. "Not one man," he wrote, "knows a prudent remedy."[58]

Not until his great novella of 1855, *Benito Cereno,* did Melville address slavery in a sustained way, although in *White-Jacket* (1850) he recounted an incident in which, as one scholar puts it, "energy is drained from the term 'slave' and channeled to the term 'sailor.' "[59] He imagined—or possibly recalled from his own experience —the feelings of a young man about to be flogged for an infraction he has not committed:

There are times when wild thoughts enter a man's heart, when he seems almost irresponsible for his act and his deed. The Captain stood on the weather-side of the deck. Sideways, on an unobstructed line with him, was the opening of the lee-gangway, where the side-ladders are suspended in port. Nothing but a slight bit of sinnate-stuff served to rail in this opening, which was cut right down to the level of the Captain's feet, showing the far sea beyond. I stood a little to windward of him, and though he was a large, powerful man, it was certain that a sudden rush against him, along the slanting deck, would infallibly pitch him headforemost into the ocean, though he who so rushed must needs go over with him. My blood seemed clotting in my veins; I felt icy cold at the tips of my fingers, and a dimness was before my eyes. But through that dimness the boatswain's mate, scourge in hand, loomed like a giant, and Captain Claret, and the blue sea seen through the opening of the gangway, showed with an awful vividness. I can not analyze my heart, though it then stood still within me. But the thing that swayed me to my purpose was not altogether the thought that Captain Claret was about to degrade me, and that I had taken an oath with my soul that he should not. No, I felt my man's manhood so bottomless within me, that no word, no blow, no scourge of Captain Claret could cut me deep enough for that. I but swung to an instinct in me—the instinct diffused through all animated nature, the same that prompts even a worm to turn under the heel. Locking souls with him, I meant to drag Captain Claret from this earthly tribunal of his to that of Jehovah, and let Him decide between us. No other way could I escape the scourge.

And then, characteristically, he derived a general principle from the particular experience:

Nature has not implanted any power in man that was not meant to be exercised at times, though too often our powers have been abused. The privilege, inborn and inalienable, that every man has, of dying himself, and inflicting death upon another, was not given us without a purpose. These are the last resources of an insulted and unendurable existence.[60]

Today this passage might evoke for us the image of a suicide bomber driven by suffering—or by a sense of solidarity with others' suffering—to use his own body as a weapon for destroying his tormentor. But in Melville's day, the incident, whether invented or factual, was clearly allusive to the plight of the slave—a prime example of what the literary scholar Carolyn Karcher has in mind when she writes that Melville "generalized about slavery by analogy."[61]

The incident in *White-Jacket* stops short of violent consummation. Thanks to a crewman who steps forward as a sort of deus ex machina to exonerate the young sailor from the charge that pushed him to the brink, there is no mutually fatal act of self-defense. There is, however, a warning of an impending *dies irae*, the day of rage that Augustine St. Clare prophesies in Harriet Beecher Stowe's abolitionist novel *Uncle Tom's Cabin* (1852). Writing before the Fugitive Slave Law inflamed both apologists and abolitionists, Melville was still able to imagine—if only barely—an intervention by which that day could be avoided or, at least, postponed.

In this respect, the passage in *White-Jacket* is strikingly cognate to one in Frederick Douglass's *Narrative of an American Slave*, first published five years earlier, in 1845, in which Douglass reflects on his decision no longer to submit but to fight off the white overseer who tries but fails to whip him and then retreats under cover of blustering threats that he will not put up with any more nigger insolence:

> This battle with Mr. Covey was the turning-point in my career as a slave. It rekindled the few expiring embers of freedom, and revived within me a sense of my own manhood. It recalled the departed self-confidence, and inspired me again with a determination to be free. The gratification afforded by the triumph was a full compensation for whatever else might follow, even death itself. He only can understand the deep satisfaction which I experienced, who has himself repelled by force the bloody arm of slavery. I felt as I never felt before. It was a glorious resurrection, from the tomb of slavery, to the heaven of freedom. My long-crushed spirit rose, cowardice departed, bold defiance took its place; and I now resolved that, however long I might remain a slave in fact, I did not hesitate to let it be known of me, that the white man who expected to succeed in whipping, must also succeed in killing me.[62]

But in the great work to which Melville turned after *White-Jacket* at the height of the Fugitive Slave Law agitation, he proved no longer willing to tell a story of violence averted. *Moby-Dick* (1851) ends not in resolution but in apocalyptic confrontation between "grand, ungodly, God-like" Ahab and the object of his unswerving vengeance, the white whale. In Ahab, Melville produced not only a timeless illustration of Tocqueville's insight that "despotism . . . presents itself as the repairer of all the ills suffered, the support of just rights, defender of the oppressed," but also a timely personification of the zealotry that was rising, in 1850–1851, on both sides of the slavery divide.[63] One measure of his success in capturing the national mood is the fact that critics have identified Ahab with that relentless foe of slavery, William Lloyd Garrison, as well as with its implacable defender, John C. Calhoun. In retrospect, Ahab seems a plausible portrait of both.

In Melville's next book, *Pierre, or the Ambiguities* (1852), he produced another portrait of implacable fury, this time of a young man whose world is blasted when he learns he has an illegitimate sister conceived in secrecy and shame by the father he had worshiped as a paragon of virtue. The blow to Pierre's innocence is compounded by his discovery that the ladies and gentlemen of his social set want to send the girl into penury or prostitution—it does not matter which, as long as she gets out of sight—so they can get on with their tidy lives. Enraged on her behalf, Pierre storms in the middle of the night into the house of his family minister (possibly modeled on the Unitarian minister Orville Dewey, a moderate anti-slavery man who defended the Fugitive Slave Law), assaulting him with questions of just the sort that abolitionists were asking on behalf of victims of that law: "*How* is she to depart? *Who* is to take her? Art *thou* to take her? *Where* is she to go? *Who* has the food for her? *What* is to keep her from the pollution to which such as she are every day driven to contribute, by the detestable uncharitableness and heartlessness of the world?" As befits the book's subtitle, it is hard to say whether Melville applauds or condemns the "vehemence, heat, and excitement" of such "harangues" (these were William Ellery Channing's words about abolitionists).[64] But the book does not end in ambiguity. It ends in utter clarity—in an orgy of madness, murder, and suicide every bit as catastrophic as the shipwreck of the *Pequod*.

As abbreviated as the foregoing readings have been, I hope they are enough to suggest a salient difference between these two writers. But Melville and Hawthorne also shared an important commonality. Both witnessed what we would call today the polarization of their country. Hawthorne hoped that moderation would prevail. Melville expected it to fail. What they had in common were, as Steven Marcus has written (about Joseph Conrad, a writer with similar preoccupations), "deep unconscious identifications with the forces of resistance and protest" as well as "a backing away and repulsion from the anticipated consequences of what such views in operation might lead to."[65] They sensed that Armageddon was coming—and that, if abolitionists and fire-eating slaveowners had their way, it would come soon.

And here, I think, is a main reason why these writers—sensitive to the crime of slavery but squeamish about the abolitionist response—became, over the course of the twentieth century, the major figures of antebellum American literature. If we pause to look at how and why they were established as such, we may gain another perspective on the history of the abolitionists' reputation.

8

One of Hawthorne's early champions was Henry James, who not only wrote the first critical biography (1879) but in a minor story, "Professor Fargo" (1874), very nearly wrote out the plot Hawthorne had proposed in his notebook about the "modern reformer" escaped from the madhouse. A decade later, in what was virtually a sequel to Hawthorne's novel about the utopian community at Brook Farm, *The Blithedale Romance* (1852), James took up in *The Bostonians* (1886) what one contemporary reviewer called "the later development" of "the abolition sentiment which prevailed in his youth."[66] For James, that sentiment was by no means a thing of the past. Like Hawthorne, he was keenly interested in the unintended consequences of philanthropic action—a theme that William Gass, in a memorable essay on *The Portrait of a Lady* (1881), called "the high brutality of good intentions."[67] In Melville's case, there was no nineteenth-century advocate of James's stature. But the twentieth-century critics who discovered and promoted him, from D. H. Lawrence to F. O. Matthiessen and Henry A. Murray, were keenly attuned to themes of ambivalence in his writing—moral and sexual as well as political.

Along with Matthiessen, the most subtle of the critics who helped establish the canon of classic American literature was Lionel Trilling, for whom literary quality was the selfsame thing as articulate ambivalence. Trilling's touchstone text was Matthew Arnold's "Dover Beach": "And we are here as on a darkling plain / Swept with confused alarms of struggle and flight, / Where ignorant armies clash by night." Beginning in the late 1930s, in essays eventually collected in his most influential book, *The Liberal Imagination* (1950), Trilling, having seen socialist ideals degraded into communist dogma, returned repeatedly to writers whom he deemed worth reading because they understood that "the highest idealism may corrupt" and may lead to crimes committed in the name of justice. Of the young protagonist in James's *The Princess Casamassima* (1886), who enlists in an anarchist cell, Trilling says he "has learned something of what may lie behind abstract ideals, the envy, the impulse to revenge and to dominance."

Trilling's work amounted to a lifelong meditation on cruelty performed in the name of truth. His controlling insight—the same I have stressed in the works of Hawthorne and Melville—was "that the moral passions are even more willful and imperious and impatient than the self-seeking passions."[68]

The point of this little excursion into the construction of literary reputation is to remind us that classic American literature of the antebellum years was defined a hundred years later by a generation of critics for whom radicalism of both left and right seemed a threat not just to political stability but to civilization itself. Many of these critics had engaged in, or at least flirted with, some form of radical politics in their youth. But having witnessed the collapse of liberal democracy in Europe, and having lived through the Great Depression when a similar prospect seemed to loom over the United States, they committed themselves, in the face of growing fervor on left and right, to what their contemporary Arthur Schlesinger Jr. called the "vital center."

That phrase, the title of Schlesinger's widely read book published in 1949, was meant to describe the narrow path between "the tyranny of the irresponsible bureaucracy" (Soviet totalitarianism), on the one hand, and "the tyranny of the irresponsible plutocracy" (unbridled corporate capitalism), on the other—between, that is, a gulag society of centralized terror and a laissez-faire society that runs on the savage principle of dog-eat-dog. "Somewhere between the abyss and the jungle" a way must be found out from between these bad alternatives—a way that would "not disrupt the fabric of custom, law and mutual confidence upon which personal rights depend." Moreover, "the transition must be piecemeal. It must be parliamentary. It must respect civil liberties and due process of law." The challenge of modernity, in other words, was to advance reform without revolution, which would be possible only within the liberal state toward which "European socialists . . . retreating . . . from the abyss of totalitarianism" and "American New Dealers advancing cautiously out of the jungle of private enterprise" were destined to converge.[69]

Written on behalf of this imperative middle way, Schlesinger's book was replete with historical commentary—on Hamiltonian versus Jeffersonian ideas of government; on the enervation of aristocracy as a coherent faction in American life; on the place of personal leadership in a world of contending interests. But nowhere did he pause for serious consideration of what today we recognize as the central historical drama of American history: the struggle over slavery. Strangely enough, one of the authorities to whom he turned in making his case for the middle way was John C. Calhoun—whom he quoted not as an exemplar but as an opponent of "wild and fierce fanaticism."[70]

In short, when mid-twentieth-century American intellectuals looked back at antebellum America, the horrors of total war commanded more of their attention than the horrors of chattel slavery—even though, as Lincoln had said in his Second Inaugural Address, "all knew" that slavery "was somehow the cause of the war." In Edmund Wilson's brilliant study of Civil War writing, *Patriotic Gore* (1962), we find William Lloyd Garrison charged with "fanaticism" and General Sherman's military tactics likened to German *Schreklichkeit* and *Blitzkrieg* as precocious examples of what today we would call state terrorism. In *The American Political Tradition* (1948), Richard Hofstadter faulted the abolitionists for having no "conception of how the slave was to be freed nor how an illiterate, landless, and habitually dependent people were to become free and self-sufficient citizens in the hostile environment of the white South."[71] He regarded the abolitionists as driven by high motives, but no more to be trusted as guides to a plausible future than the ideologues of his own time.

Looking back at antebellum America, these writers saw a world to which Yeats's haunting lines in "The Second Coming" (1919), "things fall apart / the centre cannot hold," applied with terrible precision. Their study of America's political and intellectual leadership before the Civil War revealed premonitory versions of themselves: men such as Henry Clay and, especially, Daniel Webster, who had been swept aside by the current of history for having tried and failed to defend the threatened center. In fact, Webster's prestige, mostly spent today, was so high from the 1930s to the 1950s that Stephen Vincent Benét's celebration of his eloquent patriotism, "The Devil and Daniel Webster" (1937), became a staple of grade school storybooks, and John F. Kennedy included Webster in his pantheon of Senate heroes in *Profiles in Courage* (1955; a book in which Schlesinger may have had a hand) in honor of Webster's support of the Fugitive Slave Law as the last chance to save the Union.[72]

And so American literature (broadly construed[73]) of the antebellum period came to be valued for the case it made for compromise and moderation—for the middle ground that vanished as the nation descended into fratricidal war. It was a centrism that could be retrospectively imagined but that had not been instantiated. It had been articulated in the ideal but not enacted in the actual. Its surviving expression was a literature in which the evil of slavery—shockingly, from our point of view—was virtually invisible and in which the radical enemies of slavery represented a problem more than a solution.[74]

This centrist perspective—we might call it the liberal aesthetic—could not, and did not, survive the Cold War or the concurrent academic culture wars, which, among many changes in our relation to the past, brought a fundamental recentering of American literary history. In retrospect, the opening of Kenneth Lynn's introduction to the Belknap press edition (1962) of *Uncle Tom's Cabin,* published in the same year as Wilson's *Patriotic Gore,* was a bellwether sentence: "The shame of American literature," Lynn wrote, "is the degree to which our authors of the 1830s and 1840s kept silent during the rising storm of debate on the slavery issue."[75] As I have suggested, I do not think it is quite right to say that antebellum writers stayed silent about slavery, but when they did approach the subject, they—even Melville—did so obliquely. By the mid-1960s, however, if literature was to remain part of our useable past, it could no longer be a literature that ignored, or evaded, or allegorized what Lynn rightly called "the gravest moral problem in the nation's history." It had to put the problem of slavery, and therefore the anti-slavery response, front and center. It had to be a literature that recognized, as did the abolitionists—and, for that matter, the fire-eating slaveowners—that with respect to slavery there *was* no middle way.

And so the inventory of teachable texts was both depleted and replenished. Longfellow and Whittier (though they were among those whom Lynn cited as exceptions to his rule) fell off the college reading lists. Frederick Douglass, Harriet Jacobs, Harriet Beecher Stowe, and Martin Delaney, to name just a few, came on. Those classic writers who remained were interrogated for what they knew, or refused to know, about slavery and about the men and women who committed themselves to putting an end to it. Abolitionist became a name for virtue. Anyone who balked, or lagged, or seemed wary of where abolitionist agitation might lead was consigned to the devil's party—or at least to a purgatory reserved for the timid and the weak.

9

Now that a certain exhaustion with the culture wars has set in, perhaps it is time to revisit these judgments. Already there are signs of a return to what I have called the liberal aesthetic—not, to be sure, to the cavalier disregard for the crime of slavery that deformed the work of some mid-twentieth-century critics and historians but to a certain measured sympathy for those nineteenth-century intellectual and political leaders who, although disgusted by slavery, nevertheless tried to forestall the catastrophic war they feared was coming.

Civil War scholarship seems to be turning away from the full-throated Unionism of James McPherson's *Battle-Cry of Freedom* (1988)—a book that dominated the field for some twenty years—toward a more muted assessment of the conflict as a vastly tragic, perhaps even avertable, event. I have in mind such works as Drew Faust's *This Republic of Suffering: Death and the American Civil War* (2008), which is strikingly reserved about the merits of the Union cause, and Harry S. Stout's *Upon the Altar of the Nation: A Moral History of the Civil War* (2006), which sets "aside the question of *why* the war was fought" in order to explore instead "*how* the war was fought."[76] These books focus on the devastation the war wrought or, in the case of Louis Menand's

The Metaphysical Club: A Story of Ideas in America (2001), on postwar writers who, according to Menand, repudiated the absolutist thinking in the name of which it had been waged. Another recent book, David Goldfield's *America Aflame: How the Civil War Created a Nation* (2011), portrays a nation inflamed by religious or quasi-religious passions and associates abolitionism with nativism, anti-Catholicism, and the relentless pursuit of America's Manifest Destiny, with all its fatal consequences for the American Indians who stood in its way. Echoing his teacher Avery Craven, a historian of Quaker background, whose *The Coming of the Civil War* (1966) remains a classic of the anti-war school, Goldfield goes so far as to say that "the political system established by the founders would have been resilient and resourceful enough to accommodate our great diversity sooner without the tragedy of a civil war."[77] It is, of course, an untestable assertion.

What links these books is certainly not sympathy—sneaking or otherwise—for the slave regime that abolitionists sought to destroy. Some are more frankly presentist than others (Robert Remini's *At the Edge of the Precipice: Henry Clay and the Compromise That Saved the Union* [2010] begins with the admonitory remark, plainly aimed at today's gridlock government, about "the importance of compromise in resolving problems of great magnitude in the history of our country"[78]), but all of them share a vivid awareness of the devastating consequences that followed when compromise failed. Another recent book, Mark A. Graber's *Dred Scott and the Problem of Constitutional Evil* (2006), argues that, "with different battlefield accidents," the civil war unleashed by the political failures of the 1850s "might have further entrenched and expanded human bondage."[79] In other words, we know by hindsight that one outcome of the war was the end of slavery—something that those who sought to incite or forestall it did not know, and could not have known.

Reasons for the change in tone in Civil War scholarship are not far to seek. For more than a decade, we have been living through two American-led wars that were justified, in large part, as acts of liberation on behalf of innocents living in conditions akin to slavery. Yet neither war enjoys much support among liberal-minded people professedly concerned with human rights and democratic values. My point is not to enter into the debate over "wars of choice" versus "wars of necessity" but rather to ask, if we imagine ourselves living in the America of the 1850s, how sure can we be of our judgment on the question of intervention in what people of advanced views today might call "the indigenous culture" of the South?

Would we have regarded the firing on Fort Sumter as the abolitionists did—as a welcome provocation to take up arms against an expansionist power? Or would we have regarded it as a pretext for waging war, akin to that notorious event in every baby boomer's memory, the Gulf of Tonkin incident? If we could have known in advance the scale of the ensuing carnage, would we have sided with those who considered any price worth paying to bring an end to slavery? Or would we have voted for patience, persuasion, diplomacy, perhaps economic sanctions—the alternatives to war that most liberal-minded people prefer today in the face of manifest evil in faraway lands?

Even if we agree with the historian Thomas Haskell, as I do, that the abolitionist movement spectacularly expanded "the conventional limits of moral responsibility," what were the legitimate limits of that expansion at a time when state versus national sovereignty was a matter of hot dispute?[80] Most of us live quite comfortably today with our knowledge of cruelty and oppression in nation-states whose exports are as essential to our daily lives as slave-grown cotton once was to the "free" North—yet few of us take any action beyond lamenting the dark side of "globalization." Are we sure we would have sided with those who insisted that all Americans—even if they had never seen, much less owned, a slave—had a duty forcibly to terminate the labor system of a region that many regarded, to all intents and purposes, as a foreign country? None of these questions yields an easy answer—but they should at least restrain us from passing easy judgment on those who withheld themselves from the crusade, not out of indifference but because of conscientious doubt.

Surely another reason for the shift in tone in contemporary writing about the war against slavery, though this reason may not be explicit or even fully conscious on the part of everyone on whom it exerts some effect, is the abolitionists' militant religious voice. Many abolitionists spoke and wrote in the idiom of belligerent Christianity. Harriet Beecher Stowe is said to have claimed that *Uncle Tom's Cabin* had been dictated to her by God. John Brown (whose father converted to abolitionism after reading a sermon by Jonathan Edwards Jr.) interpreted his own impending death as a kind of exemplary crucifixion. Emerson declared the gallows from which Brown was hanged as hallowed as the cross. John Jay Chapman (a "belated abolitionist," according to his friend Owen Wister) described Emerson's embrace of abolitionism as a "conversion"—though Chapman thought it was not so much "pity for the slave" as "indignation at the

violation of the Moral Law by Daniel Webster" that drove
Emerson into the arms of his new church.[81] Of Miss Birds-
eye (the old abolitionist in *The Bostonians* modeled, in part,
on Elizabeth Peabody, Hawthorne's sister-in-law), James
wrote that her "most sacred hope . . . was that she might
some day . . . be a martyr and die for something."

Through much of the twentieth century, it was reformers
such as Walter Rauschenbush, Harry Emerson Fosdick, and
Martin Luther King Jr. who held America accountable to
religious standards—men with whom secular liberals were
pleased to be associated. Today, when the language of holy
crusade has been appropriated by jihadists abroad and the
Christian right at home, the religious accent sounds a good
deal less congenial to many who deem themselves liberal or
progressive.

Other contextual changes also seem likely to influence
our sense of the past. Reading Hawthorne's judgment that
John Brown was guilty of a "preposterous miscalculation of
possibilities" in expecting his raid across the Potomac to inspire slave uprising across the South, it is hard not to think
of George W. Bush's preposterous expectation that the invasion of Iraq would be a quick operation that would trigger
a contagion of democracy throughout the Middle East. It is
equally hard to hear New York's antebellum senator, William
H. Seward, commending a "higher law" than the Constitution (the term quickly became common in abolitionist discourse, as when Henry David Thoreau demanded "men, not
of policy, but of probity—who recognize a higher law")
without thinking of former Arkansas governor Mike Huckabee's recommendation that "what we need to do, is to
amend the Constitution so it's in God's standards rather
than try to change God's standards" to fit the Constitution.

"There are constitutions and statutes, codes mercantile and codes civil," Seward declared in 1850, "but when we are legislating for states, especially when we are founding states, all these laws must be brought to the standard of the laws of God, and must be tried by that standard, and must stand or fall by it."Today these sentiments belong not to the left but to the right—and it is worth recalling that Lincoln, speaking from the shrinking center, reacted to them with "unqualified condemnation."[82]

All such historical parallels are, of course, inexact; but they are close enough, I think, to suggest that once the war against slavery had been won, America was by no means finished with its abolitionists. Nineteenth-century opponents denigrated them as "teetotalists" determined "to banish evil altogether, not to lessen or restrict it," and, in the early twentieth century, prohibitionists seized the abolitionist mantle. The editors of the *Standard Encyclopedia of the Alcohol Problem* (1928) celebrated Lincoln (portrayed as a fierce anti-slavery crusader) for his "vision of nation-wide, even world-wide triumph when there would not be one slave or drunkard in the world." In fact, the many antebellum fugitive slave narratives edited and published by abolitionists as part of the antebellum contest over public opinion provide some warrant for this view of alcoholism as a partner form of slavery—as when William Wells Brown and Henry Bibb filled their memoirs (published in 1847 and 1849, respectively) with allusions to the drink-induced savagery of the "poor and loafering class of whites" as well as of plantation masters who "loved the julep" and taught their slaves to love it, too, as a way to weaken the will to resistance and self-improvement. William Lloyd Garrison, son of an alcoholic father, published a journal warning that "Moderate Drinking

Is the Downhill Road to Intemperance and Drunkenness." Long before passage of the Eighteenth Amendment, Frederick Douglass wrote that "all great reforms go together; if we could but make the world sober, we would have no slavery." One twentieth-century prohibitionist made his case by counting "nearly twice as many slaves today"—slaves, that is, to alcohol—"than there were black men slaves in America."[83]

With this elective affinity in mind, consider this account, based on Richard Hofstadter's concept of the "paranoid style," of a persistent strain in American politics:

> The paranoid spokesman sees the world as a conflict between absolute good and absolute evil; thus social conflict is not something to be mediated or compromised; only total victory will do. He is obsessed by one subject. His particular enemy is the cause of all evil—not just some of the evils of the world, but every one of them. The enemy is the perfect model of malign intent, and yet, possibly because the enemy is a projection of self, the paranoid spokesman tends to imitate its ways.

This is a serviceable description of the abolitionist mentality (John Brown spoke of slavery as "the mother of all abominations"), but in fact it comes from Frances Fitzgerald's book about Ronald Reagan's dream of an impregnable missile shield that would make nuclear weapons "impotent and obsolete" and thereby save the world.[84]

The sacred rage of abolitionism—its moral urgency and uncompromising fervor, its vision of the world purified and perfected—has been at work in many holy wars since the war against slavery. One thinks not only of the war against drink, or of Reagan's Star Wars, but of the war against the gold standard ("You shall not crucify mankind on a cross of gold"), the "war to end all wars," the wars on poverty, on cancer, on drugs, the ongoing war on terror, and, whether we like it or not, the war against abortion—some of whose proponents, with some plausibility, see themselves as the abolitionists of our own day.

As the literary scholar Gregg Crane has shown, advocates of the higher-law standard in antebellum America believed that what begins in the individual conscience as a personal dissent from public norms will spread to the whole polity until "higher-law inspiration" is fulfilled as public consensus.[85] No matter how few and marginal the truth tellers initially may be, their seed of truth, once sown, will take root and spread against all resistance. It is God's will. This view—a kind of evangelical progressivism—which once took the form of believing that no one has the right to exercise ownership over another human being, is not fundamentally different in premise and inference from the view that no one, including the biological "owner," has the right to terminate the life of an unborn fetus. For substantive reasons concerning the advent of consciousness or the definition of personhood, or the differential impact of abortion laws on the health or life chances of poor versus affluent women, we may reject the analogy—but the structural parallels between these two forms of abolitionism seem hard to deny. Advocates for both movements range in their tactics from what the first abolitionists called "moral suasion" to armed intervention. And the parallels should remind us that all holy wars, whether metaphoric or real, from left or from right, bespeak a zeal for combating sin, not tomorrow, not in due time, not, in Lincoln's phrase, by putting it "in the course of ultimate extinction," but *now*.[86]

So it is not surprising to find one leading "pro-life" advocate describing the debate over "partial-birth" abortion as confronting "the American public with the humanity of the fetus in the same way that *Uncle Tom's Cabin* confronted the general public with the humanity of those in human bondage."[87] Early in 1851, so the story goes, Isabella Beecher wrote to her sister Harriet, "Now, Hattie, if I could use a pen as you can, I would write something that would make this whole nation feel what an accursed thing slavery is."[88] A century and a half later, a young woman attending an evangelical college asks herself, "What if you could write a book that has the same impact on abortion as *Uncle Tom's Cabin* had on slavery?," while another activist declares, after "years of talk," that "it's time to WIN this war and actually PROTECT babies with beating hearts."[89] These appropriations of anti-slavery discourse may seem forced or deluded to some of us, but that is no reason to doubt their sincerity. Why, in the view of those who believe in an inviolable right to life, should the "owner" of the fetus, any more than the owner of the slave, be exempt from the "higher law"?

It seems to me a mistake to underestimate the persistence of abolitionist sentiment as an element in American life.[90] Sometimes the abolitionist tone is stark and explicit, sometimes it is muted and implicit. One can make a case, I think, that within contemporary debates over health-care reform there lurks an incipient abolitionist idea: that behind all the clashing interest groups (pharmaceutical companies, health-care providers, insurers, and so on) there runs a current of exploitable belief that if only we could deploy enough medicine and technology, we could abolish death itself or, at least, untimely death. From this point of view, "rationing" ("pulling the plug on grandma") becomes a conspiratorial form of euthanasia perpetrated by the very government that was created to protect our rights—of which first and foremost is the right to life.[91]

More than forty years ago, Alan Harrington, brother of Michael Harrington, whose *The Other America* (1962) called for the abolition of poverty, wrote a lesser-known book, *The Immortalist* (1969), calling for the abolition of death. Its narrator concedes that the "War Against Death . . . will be an enormously complex undertaking" since it sets science against nature—against, that is, the "evolutionary plan which calls for the individual to grow, procreate and die so that the species can go on." Yet, certain that mankind will ultimately achieve true immortality, he advises "the transitional generations who still must die" to employ the stopgap measure of cryonic freezing in order to keep themselves safe till their deliverance into eternal life. It all seems preposterous. [92] To some people, every form of abolitionism has seemed preposterous—at least at first.

10

The history of abolitionist hopes and dreams—from the realistic to the fantastic—returns us to the question of what is, or ought to be, our relation to the originals who threw themselves into the war against slavery without compunction and without restraint. This seems a question to which a simple answer has to be a wrong answer. A few years ago, on the 150th anniversary of John Brown's raid, the *New York Times* published two op-ed articles commemorating the occasion. One was entitled "Freedom's Martyr," calling for a presidential pardon for a man who merits "reverence" as an American hero. The other, under the title "The 9/11 of 1859," decried Brown as a "fundamentalist" and "terrorist."[93] It is in that territory between the "yea" and the "nay" where I find myself stranded.

Anti-slavery abolitionists of the mid-nineteenth century stood outside the norms of American political practice. For many good reasons, they gave up on incremental reform and demanded a radical break from the past. They chafed within the too-long prolonged compromise of the founders, who, as the historian Leonard Levy puts it, concluded that "they could not abolish slavery and still form a strong Union" and so "did what was feasible" in their own historical moment. What that meant in practice in 1787 was taking the feasible, if feeble, step of scheduling a date (1808) by which the international slave trade would come to an end.[94] The founders also refused to acknowledge slavery by its real name in the Constitution, where it appears under the euphemism of "persons held to service," and thereby registered their hope (at least this was Lincoln's interpretation) that the day would come when slavery would cease to be a respectable institution worthy of constitutional protection.

A great deal of American historiography on the question of slavery boils down to a debate over what was "feasible" and when. Was it more feasible in the 1850s than it had been seventy years earlier to terminate slavery while preserving the nation? According to Hofstadter, abolitionists had no clue of the bloody chaos that would precede, and the depth and duration of the bitterness that would follow, their achievement of bringing slavery to an end. According to McPherson, they worked tirelessly before, and beyond, the war on behalf of their ideals—though he acknowledges that the "conversion" they wrought in the North and helped to force on the South was a fleeting one. "The emancipation of the slaves from the burden of chattel slavery," as the Southern historian Lewis P. Simpson put it, "did not emancipate the nation from the burden of slavery in other forms, including the economic and social re-enslavement of the former chattels." McPherson blames this failure on "the American people," for whom the "harsh language and moral absolutism" of the abolitionists "may have been ill-suited" as instruments of persuasion.[95]

Could compensated emancipation eventually have eased the way to abolishing slavery without the scourge of war? Could abolitionist ideals have been realized if reconstruction on the basis of racial equality had not been abandoned after the war? However one chooses to answer such counterfactual (and therefore unanswerable) questions, it should be clear enough to anyone who thinks seriously about the American past that the abolitionists made an incalculable contribution to our country and our culture. They were resoundingly right in their belief that in America a "fringe" opinion (consider the astonishing progress in women's rights and gay rights in our own time) can fast become a mainstream conviction. They set an example for subsequent reformers of the power of a determined movement to bring American reality into conformity with American ideals.

For help in illuminating the abolitionist temperament, I have turned in this essay to literature—and so it should be said that one of the legacies of abolitionism was to rescue our literature from its own complacency. It was the abolitionists who gave us the beginnings of a literature that comes from within the experience of black people rather than making outrageous inferences about their experience from without. In the eighteenth century, Thomas Jefferson noted that the slave will "sit up till midnight even though knowing he must be out with the first dawn of the morning," from which he drew the obtuse conclusion that "blacks seem to require less sleep." In the nineteenth century, Frederick Douglass wrote that "when the day's work is done, most of the slaves have their washing, mending and cooking to do," and so "many of their sleeping hours are consumed in necessary preparations of the duties of the coming day."[96] It is the difference between cant and lived truth.

Who can fail to admire those who march fearlessly into battle under the banner of "if not now, when?" And yet was there not something callow in their battle cry—the sort of insouciance that enraged William Greenleaf Eliot, a Southerner with New England roots who bravely harbored a fugitive slave in his home in St. Louis, but who, on a visit north in 1862, wrote bitterly that "the abolition Pharisees having set the house on fire rub their hands and chuckle to see how splendidly it burns"? A century later, a New Englander with Southern roots, Robert Penn Warren, echoed that sentiment with striking symmetry when he wrote that abolitionists presented "the saddening spectacle of men courageously dedicated to a worthy cause letting their nobility grow so distempered by impatience that sometimes it is difficult to distinguish love of liberty from lust for blood."[97]

Even contemporaries sympathetic to the cause thought the abolitionists underestimated the weight of history. To Eliot, they were slow to grasp the enormity of the war. To Hawthorne, who remained a friend of Charles Sumner's and, having opposed the Fugitive Slave Law, found it a "difficult and delicate" task to defend those who supported it, abolitionists failed to see how much the past constrains our ability to design the future. "We miss the good we sought," he wrote as the Civil War turned from a war for reunion into a war against slavery, "and do the good we little cared for." Future inequality—what he called "the hard battle with the world" to be fought for generations "on very unequal terms" by the descendants of slaves—was no argument to maintain present subjugation, but there was, he thought, a certain hubris in those who hail the coming of the Lord in the dawning light of today.[98]

Despite its vindicated righteousness, abolitionism still compels us to ask what is, alas, a perennial question: How much blood for how much good? In retrospect, it is an easy question. Most Americans today will not hesitate to say that the price of the Civil War, more than 600,000 dead and countless more maimed and mutilated, was well worth paying for the incipient freedom of four million. But, a century and a half after the bloodbath, this kind of easy assent is also an easy form of self-commendation. History is lived by people ignorant of the future, and surely it is a hubris of our own to dismiss all who, living in the darkness of the 1850s, made a different calculation.

I would like to close with a comment by that "belated abolitionist" John Jay Chapman, written nearly fifty years after the Fugitive Slave Law set in motion the events that would ultimately fulfill the abolitionist cause. What made Chapman different from many who have told the tale before and since is that even as he celebrated "our most blessed war" for securing the triumph of the abolitionists over the Slave Power, he recognized the tragic dignity of those who, by trying to hold some middle ground, tried to avert war while resisting them both:

> I do not know what more awful subject for a poem could have been found than that of the New England

judge enforcing the fugitive slave law. For lack of such a poem the heroism of these men has been forgotten, the losing heroism of conservatism. It was this spiritual power of a committed conscience which met the new forces as they arose, and it deserves a better name than these new forces afterward gave it.[99]

Chapman could not have known that a great poem on "the losing heroism of conservatism"—the conservatism of men such as Webster and Webster's friend Lemuel Shaw, who supported the Fugitive Slave Law despite their personal antipathy to it—had already been written. He could not have known, because Melville's valedictory masterpiece, *Billy Budd* (composed ca. 1888–1891, published 1924)—about a naval officer appalled by an unjust law, who, in order to preserve order aboard ship, carries out the prescribed capital sentence on a boy he loves—remained unpublished for another quarter century. But that, and all it implies, is another story.

2

FIGHTING THE DEVIL
WITH HIS OWN FIRE

John Stauffer

I N HIS ELEGANT ESSAY, ANDREW DELBANCO EMPHASIZES the relevance of the abolitionists for us today. Abolitionism is not only a historical subject, he argues; it is a "category of human will and sentiment—of what we might even dare to call human nature." Within this broader conceptualization, "every millenarian dreamer who has ever longed for the fire in which sin and sinners are consumed is an abolitionist—and sometimes the purification will include his own self-immolation." For Delbanco, an abolitionist is always an immediatist, "someone who identifies a heinous evil and wants to eradicate it—not tomorrow, not next year, but now." Abolitionists are idealists, and Delbanco seems to agree with Lionel Trilling, who warned that "'the highest idealism may corrupt' and may lead to crimes committed in the name of justice." Idealism is suspect, for what lies behind "abstract ideals" are less good intentions than "envy," "brutality," and "the impulse to revenge and to dominance."

In contrast to the idealism of the abolitionists, Delbanco advocates a "centrist perspective," a "liberal aesthetic," esteem for the "vital center," and an unwavering faith in the values of compromise and ambivalence. His intellectual and aesthetic heroes are men who, he argues, affirm this middle way: Hawthorne especially, but also Melville, Henry James, and Lionel Trilling.

It is a penetrating critique of the abolitionists, and it is so subtly argued that even scholars who disagree with it, as I do, cannot help but admire and respect it. Delbanco builds on a long tradition, up to the present, of uncharitable assessments of the abolitionists. As Joseph Yanielli recently noted in his 2010 prize-winning essay in the *Journal of American History,* most scholars continue to disparage white abolitionists. They call them "another permutation of the arrogant cultural imperialist, responsible for promulgating a 'proto-bourgeois' ideology." They dismiss abolitionists' efforts to empathize with slaves by arguing that such empathy was exploitative, engendering a "pornography of pain" that was both repulsive and "obscenely titillating."[1] Reading these critiques, one could easily conclude that abolitionists were more a liability than an asset to social reform. Delbanco shrewdly notes that we now "consecrate" the abolitionist *cause,* which saw slavery as an evil needing eradicating. That is true, but we are a long way from treating abolitionists with the historical empathy that they deserve.[2]

I should stress that part of my disagreement with Delbanco stems from what I perceive to be our basic philosophical differences. In his essay, Delbanco seems almost absolutist in his opposition to idealism—a kind of anti-idealist idealism—which he believes should be checked at every turn. It is an interesting perspective given that his first book is a richly sympathetic portrait of William Ellery Channing, who partly inspired the abolitionism of Charles Sumner and Henry Wadsworth Longfellow.[3]

By contrast you might call me (at least in this response) a "contextual absolutist" who believes that people's politics and worldviews can be understood and assessed only in the specific context in which they lived. In certain circumstances, centrist views are the appropriate response to political and social conditions; at other times, a conservative perspective is best; and in other instances, idealism. In the two centuries just past, however, it seems to me that idealism has been the most effective way to combat slave societies and totalitarian regimes, which dehumanized hundreds of millions of people through murder, torture, and intimidation. Slavery and totalitarianism, the dark side of the uncompromising idealism that Delbanco so richly articulates, are distinct from other evils because they foreclose compromise and preclude the possibility of a middle way. In such circumstances, one needs to fight violent fanatics with a more humane fanaticism—a central aim of most abolitionists and Nazi resisters.

I also disagree with Delbanco's assessment that idealism and utopian thought necessarily, or even typically, lead to corruption, brutality, and the impulse to revenge and dominance. Indeed Delbanco ignores the fact that the first organized group of abolitionists were the Quakers—idealists, pacifists, and prophets believing in the Inner Light—who tempered their perfectionism with a sense of humility before God and their fellow humans. As many scholars have noted, Quakers were compromisers: they continually compromised their perfectionist impulses and abided by the laws of their society.[4]

Then, too, Delbanco's embrace of a liberal aesthetic and centrist point of view seems to me to be a largely *white* aesthetic and point of view.[5] With the exception of Melville, his antidotes to the abolitionists—chiefly Hawthorne but also James and Trilling—either refuse to acknowledge the plight of blacks or virtually ignore their presence in American society. Let me offer a few examples of Hawthorne's, James's, and Trilling's comparative blindness with regard to race and slavery.[6]

One of the most incisive judgments of Hawthorne's attitude toward blacks comes from his friends, Henry Wadsworth Longfellow and Longfellow's wife Fanny. In an 1851 letter to Henry, Hawthorne writes:

> How glad I am that [Charles] Sumner is at last elected [to the U.S. Senate]! Not that I ever did, nor ever shall, feel any preeminent ardor for the [anti-slavery] cause which he advocates, nor could ever have been moved, as you were, to dedicate poetry[7]—or prose either—to its advancement. There are a hundred modes of philanthropy in which I could blaze with intenser zeal.[8]

Fanny responds by saying that Hawthorne's "sympathies are absorbed by the sufferings of his own race, but a large heart can hold all."[9] It is a brilliant summary of Hawthorne's reform sensibilities: he sympathizes with the sufferings of whites but not blacks. Abolitionists like herself, her husband, and Sumner have larger hearts that can reach out to *all* humans.

Fanny's critique of Hawthorne's hard-heartedness is supported by Hawthorne's own writings on blacks. In 1846 his close friend Horatio Bridge, a naval officer who was patrolling the African coast, participated in a skirmish with some Africans. Hawthorne urged him to stay on board ship and avoid fighting Africans: "A civilized and educated man must feel somewhat like a fool, methinks, when he has staked his own life against that of a black savage, and lost the game. In the sight of God, one life may be as valuable as another; but in our view, the stakes are very unequal."[10] Hawthorne ignores the scriptural message, embraced by abolitionists, that "God is no respecter of persons" (in God's eyes all humans are equal).[11] Instead he invokes his own adage: black savages are "very unequal" to educated white men in their basic humanity.

These attitudes toward blacks help explain Hawthorne's view of American slavery in his 1852 presidential biography of his friend and Southern sympathizer Franklin Pierce. Near the end of the book, Hawthorne agrees with Pierce by saying that the evil of abolition agitation "was certain, while the good was, at best, a contingency." Hawthorne adds that blacks and whites in the South "now dwelt together in greater peace and affection, it is not too much to say, *than had ever elsewhere existed* between the taskmaster and the serf." He defended these sentiments two months after his biography was published. "What I [said in Pierce's biography] on the slavery question . . . are my real sentiments, and I do not now regret that they are on record."[12]

For Hawthorne, then, slavery was a comparatively benign institution. No wonder he refused to take a stand against it. No wonder, too, that from the 1850s until his death in 1864, he (along with his friend Franklin Pierce) remained loyal to the Democratic Party, even when it was shaped by Southerners and after secession "tarred with the brush of treason." During the war, Hawthorne advocated "amputation," hoping that the Confederacy would remain a separate slaveholding nation.[13] This is precisely what Confederates desired, and it helps explain why the Lincoln administration called such Copperhead views "treasonous." Indeed Northern Democratic editors and leaders received money and support from the Confederacy. In January 1864, Confederate Secretary of State Judah P. Benjamin, who oversaw intelligence operations, was told "that it would be worthwhile for him to get in touch with ex-president [Franklin] Pierce."[14] One final intimation of Hawthorne's Southern sympathies: during the war he requested an autograph of Jefferson Davis but not one of Abraham Lincoln.[15]

Henry James was considerably more sympathetic to the plight of blacks and abolitionists than was Hawthorne. His brother Wilky served as an officer in the 54th Massachusetts Colored Regiment and was badly injured in the attack on Fort Wagner. "Our sympathies, our own as a family's, were all enlisted on behalf of the race that had sat in bondage," Henry recalled.[16]

James had immense respect for Charles Sumner, a leading abolitionist, friend of numerous blacks, and vigorous champion of racial equality. In his 1903 book on William Whetmore Story, a sculptor and friend of Sumner, James calls Sumner an exemplary statesman and patriot, "signally eloquent" in denouncing Southern statesmen, and a "generous friend" whose letters were "irresistible" and among the "best" of the era. James went so far as to say that the South's firing on Fort Sumter constituted "but the *second* shot of the war," the first being Preston Brooks's "merciless" caning of Sumner on the Senate floor, "which was like a welt raised by the lash itself across the face of the North." James so admired Sumner that in his biography the abolitionist overshadows the artist.[17]

But after the war James's sympathies toward blacks waned, much as they did for so many other intellectuals.[18] When he returned to the United States after living abroad for almost thirty years, his writings accommodated "the full-scale retreat of the North from support of black equal rights," according to Kenneth Warren. For example, he favorably reviewed William Dunning's *Essays on the Civil War and Reconstruction* (1898), a foundational text in the influential "Dunning school" of American historiography, which bemoaned the "abasement" of Southern states' rights and the rise of political and legal rights for blacks during Reconstruction. James not only agrees with Dunning's history; he calls it "irresistible to read" and is so taken with it that he finds himself "sometimes holding my breath."[19]

The American Scene (1907) constitutes James's most sustained attempt to grapple with American race relations. In it he calls Du Bois's *The Souls of Black Folk* "the only Southern book of any distinction published for many a year." But it is a "backhanded compliment," since James dismisses all Southern literature and culture as torpid and horribly dull. "How . . . can everything so have gone?" he wonders. He blames the dire state of Southern culture on the "intimate presence of the Negro" coupled with the "lingering effects of a slave society."[20] More significantly, he ignores the culture of lynching and intimidation that kept blacks unfree. And despite his brilliant and lifelong efforts to represent consciousness and subjectivity through his art, he makes no effort to understand black subjectivity. Silence was James's preferred mode for improving race relations. As Warren summarizes, "James's contribution to the discourse of race in America is at best ambivalent"—and here "ambivalence" is not meant to be an admirable trait.[21]

Lionel Trilling helped establish Hawthorne and James as foundational figures in the American canon, and he is not only the best known New York intellectual but one of the most important cultural critics of the twentieth century. Like James and Hawthorne, he remained largely silent about the plight of blacks in America, and more generally he neglected the role of power and coercion in shaping society. "A society like ours, despite some appearances to the contrary, tends to be seductive rather than coercive," he said.[22] Although Trilling was a public intellectual who critiqued numerous social and political issues of his day, one can read his corpus and never know that the civil rights movement, which coincided with his career, even occurred. Indeed, in an important new book, Michael Kimmage argues that Trilling needs to be appreciated as a major contributor to the rise of neoconservatism. A self-described anti-communist liberal, Trilling helped push liberal intellectuals toward a center that was itself becoming much more conservative beginning in the 1950s. While he dismissed conservatives as irrelevant, he persistently and subtly attacked the "vulgar radicalism" and "adversary culture" of the left. The effect was to open "the door to conservative ideas" among liberal intellectuals. Kimmage brilliantly describes a neoconservative convergence of Trilling and Whittaker Chambers, a former fellow traveler turned anti-communist conservative. He shows how Trilling's writings, especially his 1947 novel, *The Middle of the Journey,* were blueprints "for the cultural reversal that became known as neoconservatism."[23]

In upholding Hawthorne, James, and Trilling as moral and political antidotes to the abolitionists, it seems to me that Delbanco makes the same mistake as Trilling in confusing the relationship between art and politics. Trilling wanted "to make 'the aesthetic the criterion of the moral' and political."[24] But as the critic Joseph Frank shrewdly noted,

> it is one thing to make the experience of art—the experience of pleasure and beauty, of harmony and reconciliation—the ideal form of moral life. It is quite another to attribute the virtues of this aesthetic ideal to concrete social behavior. . . . In other words, it is of the

utmost importance not to confuse the boundaries of the ideal and the real, the aesthetic and the social; not to endow social passivity and quietism *as such* with the halo of aesthetic transcendence.[25]

We can love and cherish the art of Hawthorne, James, and Trilling (or any artist, for that matter) and yet also acknowledge that their moral views and politics were something wholly different and less than desirable models for action.

In contrast to Hawthorne, James, and Trilling, Melville grappled with race and identified with the plight of blacks more deeply than did most of his peers. But he was also horrified by the growing sectional polarization; the crisis over the meaning of the Constitution; the widespread repudiation of the rule of law by Northerners and Southerners; and the unknown costs of freedom. Melville understood the degree to which violence would beget more violence, and I found Delbanco's assessment of him superb—Delbanco is one of Melville's preeminent critics and biographers. He neatly distinguishes between Hawthorne's and Melville's liberal aesthetic by saying that while "Hawthorne hoped that moderation would prevail," Melville "expected it to fail." Given that Melville got it right, I wish that Delbanco had given more weight to Melville in his essay. Indeed a more persuasive group of writers and critics, who conform to Delbanco's "liberal aesthetic" but who also confronted directly the problems of race and slavery, would begin with Melville and include Twain, Hurston, Faulkner, and Ellison.

Part of the reason why Melville got it right in assuming that moderation and compromise would fail is because, unlike

Hawthorne, he did not elide or ignore blacks in his writings. He had a far better understanding of the power of slavery and race in the country than did Hawthorne. Melville understood what the opponents of slavery were up against, and I wish Delbanco would have developed this point, framing his critique of the abolitionists in relation to their enemies. Doing so would have revealed the degree to which Southern elites, far more than the abolitionists, were the uncompromising idealists and aggressors. In what follows, I develop this point, reframing the narrative in order to show what the abolitionists were up against and how they responded to the spread of slavery.

From the Constitutional Convention in 1787 until the 1820s, almost every abolitionist, black and white, sought *gradual* abolition through peaceful and legal means. These early abolitionists were far from fanatics; they were respected national leaders. In 1790 Benjamin Franklin was president of the Pennsylvania Abolition Society, while Alexander Hamilton, John Jay, and Gouverneur Morris led the New York Abolition Society. Paul Cuffe and James Forten were highly successful and respected black businessmen, and Cuffe was the first African American to meet with and advise a U.S. president.[26]

These early abolitionists were representative of America's elites. Although most of America's founders and framers were slaveowners—from Thomas Jefferson, George Washington, James Madison, and Charles Pinckney to John Jay, John Hancock, Benjamin Franklin, and Gouverneur Morris—the vast majority of them were also genuinely anti-slavery. They sought a gradual end to the evil without uprooting the social order or their own wealth and domestic comforts. Madison, the architect of the Constitution and himself a slaveholder, called slavery America's "original sin," a sentiment shared by most leaders of the early Republic.[27]

The early abolitionists were influenced by the Enlightenment ideals of natural rights, which embraced the idea of self-sovereignty for all adults, coupled with a clearly defined social hierarchy. African American leaders helped popularize beliefs in individual freedom. They urged white leaders to broaden the concept of citizenship so that they, too, could enjoy the inalienable right to freedom and property. And they tried to loosen the rigid social hierarchy.[28]

In many respects, this early abolition movement was a conservative response to slavery. The first abolition societies did not challenge existing racial hierarchies. Indeed they refused to accept African Americans as members. Even the Quakers did not welcome blacks into their churches and homes. Many, perhaps most, of the early abolition leaders, including African Americans such as Paul Cuffe and for a while Richard Allen and James Forten, advocated emigration to Africa—though not through the American Colonization Society when it emerged in 1816—as a pragmatic solution to racism and slavery. These "black founders," along with white leaders, emphasized prudence rather than defiance as a strategy for ending slavery.[29]

Most abolitionists were "firmly in the camp" of the elitist Federalist Party. This preference reflected Federalists' advocacy of a clearly defined social hierarchy that emphasized universal freedom and a strong central government rather than equality. Elite whites wanted blacks to rise up and become free but not equal. According to this perspective, blacks would remain at or near the bottom of the social order or be shipped to another country, thus posing little threat to the elite's own white identities.[30]

This early abolition movement was hugely successful. It led to the abolition of slavery in the Northern states; the exclusion of slavery in the Northern territories; the voluntary manumission of some 20,000 slaves by their masters by 1800, mostly in Southern states; a dramatic rise in the population of free blacks; and the end of the international slave trade. Abolitionists believed, like their counterparts throughout the New World, that ending the African trade would be a crucial first step toward ultimate extinction. Many did not realize that the United States was virtually unique as a slave society: the slave population reproduced naturally, whereas elsewhere in the New World, deaths exceeded births and planters depended on continual imports from Africa to sustain their labor force and profits.[31]

Another indication of the success of the early abolition movement is the degree to which Northerners and Southerners worked together in their hopes to end slavery everywhere in the nation. A basic agreement existed between Northern and Southern statesmen: the North would not interfere with slavery in Southern states; and Southerners would recognize slavery as an evil that should be discouraged and eventually abolished.[32]

This rational and pragmatic approach was smart politics. Slavery was being abolished, free soil was spreading, and the leading statesmen "professed to believe that chattel slavery . . . must inevitably give way to Christian freedom."[33] Black abolitionists also had reason to believe in linear progress and to assume that slavery would gradually end throughout the nation. After all, practical and nonviolent measures for ending slavery seemed to be working. Moreover, many blacks could remember the bloodshed and upheaval of the Revolution, and they strategically chose to compromise with slavery's sin by accepting gradual means to prevent more bloodshed.[34]

In short, these early abolitionists endorsed all of Delbanco's liberal values: they compromised effectively and worked across sectional, and occasionally racial, divisions. They embraced a "centrist" perspective and a "vital center" that called for the ultimate extinction of slavery. And they were staunch supporters of a rational social order and the rule of law.

This brief history of the early abolition movement raises a crucial question: what happened? Why did the "gradual" abolitionists of the early Republic evolve into the "immediatist" abolitionists beginning in the 1830s? Why did the nation become so sectionally polarized? The short answer is the rise of King Cotton and unprecedented profits from slave labor, coupled with a sudden belligerence among slaveowning Southerners, who, feeling threatened by the success of emancipation movements throughout Europe and the New World, began to look for ways to expand slavery.[35]

The Missouri Compromise was a crucial turning point that destroyed the successes of the early abolition movement. When the House of Representatives debated a bill that would allow Missouri to enter the Union as a slave state, the New York representative James Tallmadge proposed an amendment that would gradually abolish slavery there. The ensuing debate erupted "like a firebell in the night," as Thomas Jefferson noted, and became known as the "Missouri crisis." For many statesmen, the fate of slavery in the new nation hinged on whether Missouri would be a free or slave state. Many Southern leaders threatened to secede. Henry Clay negotiated a compromise that allowed Missouri to enter the Union as a slave state while prohibiting the spread of slavery north of the 36° 30' parallel within the former Louisiana

Purchase territory. While most Northerners viewed the compromise as a victory for the South, many Southerners sowed seeds of future division by arguing that the provision restricting the spread of slavery conceded too much to the North and gave unwarranted power to Congress.[36]

The Missouri Compromise marked the beginning of a transformation in American society. It pointed to signs of a new era in reform, including a shift in visions of citizenship and community and in definitions of national and cultural boundaries. This transformation took many forms: the emergence of a national market economy; rapid westward expansion, which became the battleground of slavery; and a blurring of God's law and national law. During the Missouri crisis, the New York politician and reformer Rufus King was the first politician to invoke a "higher law" in reference to slavery; he stated that any law upholding slavery was "absolutely void, because [it is] contrary to the law of nature, which is the law of God." King stunned both Northern and Southern colleagues by interpreting the Constitution through an abstract reading of the principles of freedom and equality in the Declaration of Independence. The higher law thesis would become a central rhetorical weapon in the writings of a later generation of black and white abolitionists.[37]

Most significantly, the Missouri crisis marked a moment in which Americans became increasingly unwilling to compromise with sin and to accept limits, the rule of law, and traditional boundaries in their quest to realize visions of a new age. After the Missouri Compromise, the basic agreement between the North and South over the fate of slavery became untenable. Over the course of the 1820s, Southerners affirmed pro-slavery ideology, repudiated the belief, shared by most of their forebears, that slavery was a sin, and began to envision an empire of slavery. In response, the North witnessed the rise of "modern" or immediate abolitionism, as it was called by both blacks and whites, which distinguished itself from the earlier generation of abolitionists in its understanding that gradual measures only played into the hands of aggressive slaveowners. Increasingly, abolitionists' most passionate desire was the immediate end of all sin, and they saw slavery as the bolt around which all other evils swung.[38]

But these desires did not mean that immediatists were unwilling to compromise. To be sure, some men, such as William Lloyd Garrison, were comparatively unyielding in their refusal to compromise with sin and their adherence to specific ideals. But as a group, the abolitionists proposed numerous strategies in the hopes of working with Southerners to end slavery. These measures included the desire for lawful debate; the use of moral suasion, including millions of anti-slavery petitions to Congress and the proliferation of anti-slavery writings and images in newspapers, pamphlets, and broadsides; numerous proposals for compensated emancipation, which Southerners totally ignored; boycotts of slave-grown products; international pressure, especially from Great Britain, in the hopes of bringing Southerners to the bargaining table; slave resistance (especially running away) and the specter of slave rebellions—what Frederick Douglass and Herman Melville both called "a slumbering volcano" blanketing the South; a sophisticated Underground Railroad; and the emergence of anti-slavery political parties, in which immediatists worked closely with gradualists to end slavery through peaceful and constitutional channels. Much like the early gradual abolition movement, nonviolence was the foundation of the modern immediatist movement, though not every immediatist adhered to that ideal.[39]

In the broadest sense, the Missouri crisis induced a national rite of passage reflecting a move away from "gradualism" and toward "immediatism." This shift was linked to signs that the old Republic, defined by Enlightenment beliefs, was disappearing, and that a new empire (masquerading as a republic), defined by Romantic worldviews, was emerging.[40]

Unlike the popularity of the earlier gradualist movement, immediate abolitionists remained a tiny minority up to the eve of the Civil War. In part this was because they advocated universal freedom and racial equality and many of them took steps toward realizing these egalitarian ideals. *Pace* Delbanco, they defined themselves against the American Colonization Society, vigorously opposing it as racist.[41]

The immediatist movement brought blacks and whites together as friends and allies in ways that had never occurred before in America. Abolitionists created the nation's first integrated communities, despite the rise of racism and the hardening of racial hierarchies, provoking mob violence against the abolitionists.[42]

In essence, the liberal abolitionists of the early Republic became the colonizationists and "liberal" anti-slavery advocates of the antebellum era. They distanced themselves from the radical immediatists. Although their enemies tried to stain them with abolitionism, or "black Republicanism," they rarely defined themselves as such.

Then, too, Southerners staged a "counter-revolution" beginning in the 1820s, as Manisha Sinha, William Freehling, and David Davis have emphasized. It was a conservative, anti-democratic movement to protect and perpetuate racial slavery. By the early 1830s, after Nat Turner's rebellion, the inauguration of Garrison's *Liberator,* and South Carolina's failed attempt to nullify federal law, Southern states refused to tolerate any form of dissent against their "peculiar institution." They created what the Southerner James Silvers called "a closed society." And they led the way in transforming society based on their own version of "higher law" ideals. They invoked a higher law than the Constitution that made slavery sacrosanct; and they effectively revoked the constitutional freedoms of speech, petition, debate, assembly, and due process in matters threatening white supremacy. They imposed "Gag Rules" in Congress, which for eight years automatically tabled all discussion of slavery. A number of Southern states offered up to $5,000 as a reward for the arrest and extradition of leading abolitionists to be tried for libel; and Southern newspapers published blacklists of banned, anti-slavery writings. John C. Calhoun vainly tried to pass a federal law banning the circulation of all abolitionist writings and images. While pro-slavery Southerners could travel and speak throughout the North without incident, if an anti-slavery Northerner went south, his life was in jeopardy.[43]

The rise of immediatism, or "modern abolition," as it was sometimes called, was thus a response to Southern revolutionaries who suddenly sought an empire for slavery. For example, John Quincy Adams, the former president and son of John Adams, and in one sense the last Founding Father, began to define himself as an abolitionist as a result of Southerners' growing belligerence. As a congressman in the 1830s, he received periodic death threats for his fierce opposition to slavery. He drew on his deep knowledge of the Constitution to argue, beginning in 1836, that "in case of war," the federal government could, through the "war power" clause, legally abolish slavery in the states. And he maintained that "the people had a right to reform abuses of the government" in order to align it with the ideals of the Declaration. For this he was formally censured and accused of treason. By the early 1840s, after withstanding constant "insult, bullying," and "death threats" from slaveholders, he began calling himself an abolitionist. He said his conversion stemmed from John C. Calhoun's "open and brazen avowals" to acquire Texas and perpetuate slavery. "When I see the Constitution of my country struck down by the South, . . . no alternative is left me" than to become an abolitionist, he said. "I must oppose them [Southerners] with all the means within my reach. I must fight the devil with his own fire." Adams's conversion suggests that a "vital center" no longer existed in the nation. Southerners had hijacked the original intentions of the founders.[44]

By the late 1850s, Southerners had succeeded in nationalizing slavery. In his "House Divided" speech, Lincoln accurately stated that Southern leaders were conspiring against the United States government in their quest to extend slavery into every territory and state. Indeed, Lincoln warned of another Supreme Court decision, a "second Dred Scott," that would open every state to slavery. Soon Northern cities would be filled with slaveowners and their slaves. This was not some crazy conspiracy theory or "paranoid style." Proslavery judges and lawyers had argued that the Dred Scott decision of 1857 protected slaveholders' property if they moved to free states. And a "second Dred Scott" case—*Lemon v. People*—was working its way through the courts. It invoked the right of transit, demanding respect for Southerners' "property" when they brought their slaves north, as Paul Finkelman has emphasized. Simultaneously, powerful slaveowners sought ways to annex Cuba and parts of Central

America in their efforts to realize their ideals of a slave empire. Many also tried to reopen the African slave trade, and illegal slave traders dared the federal government to try to catch them.[45]

Indeed had there been no immediate abolition movement, Southerners might have fulfilled Lincoln's warning in his "House Divided" speech: slavery would have become "lawful in *all* the States, *old* as well as *new—North* as well as *South*." And they probably would have succeeded in their dreams of annexing parts of Central America. Such a scenario could well have proved the death knell to the New World emancipation movement. According to Seymour Drescher, American abolitionists greatly energized abolitionists in Brazil and helped bring about peaceful abolition there. In 1858 Lincoln believed that the "ultimate extinction" of slavery through gradual means would occur in the United States in not "less than at hundred years at the least"—1958 at the earliest. He was not alone in his estimation that a peaceful and gradual end to chattel slavery would require at least a century. But he, like most other anti-slavery advocates and political abolitionists, recognized that Southerners sought to reverse the progress of emancipation in the New World.[46]

Secession underscored the anti-democratic nature of Southern revolutionaries. The war came because Southern politicians refused to accept a democratically elected president who, while calling slavery evil and seeking to prohibit its spread, vowed not to touch slavery in the slave states. In his inaugural address, Lincoln tried to conciliate with Southerners and went so far as to endorse a newly passed constitutional amendment—the first Thirteenth Amendment (it was never ratified)—that guaranteed slavery in the slave states *forever*.[47]

In his inaugural address, Lincoln succinctly summarized the central issue dividing the country: "One section of our country believes slavery is *right,* and ought to be extended, while the other believes it is *wrong,* and ought not to be extended. This is the only substantial dispute." No one disagreed with him on this point.[48] One month later, when the U.S. government tried to send food to starving soldiers stationed at a federal fort, Southerners bombed it for two days, starting the war.

The belligerence of Southern leaders did not end with Appomattox. They neither laid down their arms nor accepted the terms of their unconditional surrender. Instead, they went home and engaged in a terrorist war for the next twelve years. They lost the fight to preserve their new nation and the chattel slavery on which it was based. The Confederacy was defeated, but ironically, despite the devastation they suffered, Southerners won the war in the sense that they preserved black unfreedom in new forms that were in some ways "worse than slavery," as David Oshinsky and others have noted.[49] In 1877, after the federal government withdrew the remaining federal troops from the South, the Northern writer and lawyer Albion Tourgée, who had himself recently returned from the South, offered this shrewd assessment of the war: "The way in which the South has reversed the verdict of Appomattox is the grandest thing in American politics."[50]

In a profound respect, then, the limitations of the abolitionists were even greater than Delbanco suggests. For although they helped end chattel slavery, they utterly failed in their goals of achieving universal freedom and equality before the law. Most white abolitionists and Northerners, in their desire for reunion, forgave the Rebels, believing that

Confederates would acknowledge their sins and repent. Few of them understood the degree to which Southerners sought to "redeem" themselves by retaliating against blacks and Republicans.[51] As Delbanco implies in his poignant ending, no one could have foreseen the degree to which the century of horrible racial oppression following the war stemmed in part from the violence that brought slavery to an end.[52]

A few contemporaries did predict the future. In *Moby-Dick* Melville brilliantly warns of the apocalyptic costs of denying limits, ignoring rules, and refusing to compromise. When Ahab destroys the quadrant, he symbolically destroys the instrument of knowledge and rationality that should determine his place in the cosmos. Like Ahab pursuing the whale, Americans found in pro-slavery and abolitionist visions, along with other monomaniacal pursuits, the means to strike through the pasteboard masks of visible objects and seek to realize their utopian ideals.[53] The abolitionists, however, were far more willing than their pro-slavery counterparts to oppose violent means and compromise their utopian impulse.

Indeed Melville was such a prescient and powerful writer that one might be provocative and go so far as to say that if every American had been required to read *Moby-Dick* when it was published in 1851, the Civil War may have been avoided. And if slavery had been abolished without the bloodbath of war, race relations today would no doubt be much different, and probably far better. But that of course begs the question of how slavery could have ended peacefully. To this conundrum no one yet has provided a compelling answer.[54]

3

DID THE ABOLITIONISTS
CAUSE THE CIVIL WAR?

Manisha Sinha

A NDREW DELBANCO'S REEVALUATION OF ABOLITIO-
nism in Chapter 1 is a restrained but nonetheless
pointed critique of what one might call the abolitionist *mentalité*. Drawing on the works of Nathaniel Hawthorne and Herman Melville, he questions the value of abolitionist contributions to the struggle against slavery, which
resulted in a long, destructive war. In doing so, he grants abolitionists and their opponents, much to the former's disadvan-
tage, the benefits of historical hindsight. The major problem
confronting antebellum Americans was racial slavery and not
the movement against it. Abolitionists addressed the cancer
at the heart of the slaveholding American republic; they did
not invent it. Delbanco identifies abolitionism as an extremist
trend in American history, a "recurrent American phenomenon" or a "persistent impulse in American life,"[1] that in its
uncompromising opposition to a problem (slavery) brings on
greater evil (war). One might argue instead that the persistent
and recurrent problem in American history has been racial
inequality. Far from deserving the vast condescension of posterity, abolitionists were prophetic in first developing this
insight.

The roots of Delbanco's assessment lie in an old and entrenched historiography that caricatured abolitionists as

fanatical, unreasonable, and extreme in their views. The long-standing historical demonization of abolitionists stemmed from unsympathetic contemporary reactions to them as "monomaniacs" in the North or as "incendiaries" in the overblown rhetoric of the South. A recent historian has gone so far as to anachronistically label abolitionists "terrorists" and reproduce uncritically the perspectives of Southern slaveholders. Not surprisingly, abolitionists in this reading are meddlesome outsiders forcing slaveholders from the supposedly anti-slavery Virginians to the rabidly pro-slavery South Carolinians into a defense of slavery resting on the allegedly "paternalistic" relationship between masters and slaves.[2]

The idea of aggressive abolitionists and a defensive slave South is old hat despite its surprising recent resurgence. It not only recasts the actual history of an assertive and powerful slaveholding class, who easily bent law, politics, custom, and men to serve their interests in pre–Civil War America. But it also buys into the stereotype of "little abolitionist orators," haranguing Americans on slavery in the "church and school basements," as traitors to reason, tradition, and even nature. Abolitionist motivation was often assigned to psychological pathology, status anxiety, religious enthusiasm, or moral rigidity, and what philosophers call the principle of charity was completely missing in an understanding of the movement. It had an influential counterpart in popular culture and literature, especially in the novels of Henry James, where abolitionists were commonly portrayed as unlikeable, self-righteous do-gooders, direct descendants of an even more unlikeable, intolerant bunch, those witch-burning, dour Puritans in pointy hats. While Perry Miller, Edmund Morgan, and Delbanco himself have done much to bust the popular myths associated with Puritanism at least in the academy, abolitionists, it seems, still need vindication.[3]

Countless southern-inspired revisionist histories of the coming of the Civil War blamed fanatical minorities for starting a "needless" war. According to this interpretation, abolitionists were a determined, dangerous minority, who managed to plunge the nation into war. Of course, such a view is predicated on the complete historical erasure of African Americans, enslaved and free, and their perspectives. It also minimized the enormity of the issues facing the slave-holding republic in the mid-nineteenth century.[4] At a time when history, the pseudoscience of race, and literature conspired to undo the emancipatory results of the Civil War and Reconstruction, unsympathetic views of abolitionists became dominant and entrenched. Historian Rayford Logan long ago dubbed this period the "nadir" in African American history, when disfranchisement, segregation, lynching, sharecropping, and debt peonage made a mockery of black freedom. Abolitionists and their anti-slavery allies in the North may have won the war, but former slaveholders and their conservative allies won the peace. The tragedy of American history is not that the abolitionist vision briefly triumphed over inertia and conservatism but that the conservative critics of the abolitionists, of their moral urgency and radical devotion to African American rights, plunged the nation into yet another long racial nightmare. As W. E. B. Du Bois pointed out, the slave stood briefly in the sun before being shoved back into the shadows.[5]

Delbanco provides us with an adeptly argued version of the revisionist history of abolition and the Civil War. For him, arriving at a more balanced appraisal of the abolition movement rests on taking seriously northern conservatives' critique of abolition or the abolitionist mindset. Despite attempts by a handful of "nationalist" historians, abolitionists, their children, and African American writers and historians such as Archibald Grimké and Du Bois to write a different narrative of the movement, the heroic portrayal of abolitionists as freedom fighters did not take hold until as late as the 1960s. When civil rights activists looked for historical precedents, they naturally saw themselves as heirs to the abolitionist struggle against slavery and for black rights and called for a Second Reconstruction. The alleged "consecration" of the abolition cause, however, has been relatively short-lived, often dismissed as "neo-abolitionist" history.

Critical views of abolitionists that resurfaced quickly are often mired in contradictions that are apparent in Delbanco's essay. According to this view, abolitionists are an insignificant "bitter" minority, yet powerful enough to cause the nation's most destructive war. They are radical yet conservative. Even more problematic is the conclusion that holds abolitionists responsible for all the failures of emancipation but denies them credit for its enactment. Criticism from the right blames abolitionists for their irresponsible, anti-institutional, and destructive politics or, from the left, for their supposedly bourgeois and essentially conservative agenda.[6]

Abolition, though, was hardly a stalking horse for capitalism, nor were Southern slaveholders, *pace* Eugene Genovese, capitalism's staunchest critics. In fact, most pro-slavery theorists defended the right to property with an ardor that would put to shame its bourgeois adherents. Many of them, like James Henry Hammond of South Carolina, were reactionary critics of free labor society arguing that labor must be enslaved to prevent mischief. This, needless to say, was not much of a socialist solution to the plight of free labor.

Or as another South Carolinian worthy James Chesnut put it, "red republicanism" in America had merely "blacked its face." Marx himself pointed out that there could be no working class movement in the United States as long as the black half of it remained enslaved, an assessment with which most abolitionists at least agreed.[7]

Indeed, abolitionist characterization of slavery as an especially egregious instance of oppression is bolstered rather than vitiated in the incident related by Delbanco (see Chapter 1, note 4). Here he recounts Hammond's paternalistic concern for his slave son who was ill treated by the new master to whom the boy had been sold. The striking fact here is not that Hammond intervened on behalf of his son but that he sold him. Despite his high-sounding defense of slavery, Hammond was a lecherous freak who abused not only many of his slave women but probably his own slave daughter and, in a spectacular political scandal, his white nieces. This man was successively a governor, congressman, and senator from his state. Hammond's many cruel and pathetic attempts to gain absolute mastery over his slave labor force aptly illustrated the abolitionist indictment of slaveholding. As the abolitionist, clergyman, and former slave James W. C. Pennington argued, slavery in any form was indefensible because it was based on "the chattel principle," the reducing of human beings to property or marketable commodities. Talk of Christian, benevolent, and paternalistic masters, he wrote, sickened him.[8]

Delbanco, though, is hardly a latter-day apologist for slavery, nor does his work suffer from the most obvious omissions of the earlier generation of revisionist historians of the Civil War. It is important, then, to consider his argument that conservative opponents of abolitionists may have had a point and that they correctly predicted the bloody cost of internecine warfare. Delbanco arrives at his conclusion through an engaging analysis of literature; I will challenge it through the lens of history.

At the very outset, it is important that we differentiate between abolitionists and those who were anti-slavery in sentiment, a distinction that the dean of historians of slavery and abolition, David Brion Davis, insisted on a long time ago.[9] A failure to do so results in William Ellery Channing popping up both as a "prophet" of abolition and as a critic of abolitionists in Delbanco's essay. Most historians reserve the term "abolitionists" for the second phase of abolition directed against Southern slavery during the antebellum period, ignoring the first wave of emancipation in the Northern states in the age of the American Revolution. Even if we define abolitionists at a very rudimentary level, as people devoted to ending slavery from the Revolution to the Civil War, many if not most pretenders to the title would fall off the bandwagon.

During the Revolutionary era, African American efforts to challenge slavery through petitions, freedom suits, fighting on both sides of the War of Independence, running away, and eventually abandoning the country of their enslavement belong much more to the annals of abolition than do the ineffectual hand-wringing of a few slaveholders. The anti-slavery reputation of slaveholding republicanism, as black abolitionists would later point out, was highly overrated. In fact, these abolitionists did not hesitate to take on that pre-eminent exemplar of American republicanism, Thomas Jefferson, whose acute racism they argued vitiated his anti-slavery. For David Walker, ideas about black racial inferiority "having emanated from Mr. Jefferson, a much greater philosopher the world never afforded, has in truth injured us more, and has been as great a barrier to our emancipation as anything that has ever been advanced against us." African Americans, he argued, must refute Jefferson as "his remarks respecting us, have sunk deep into the hearts of millions of whites, and never will be removed this side of eternity." And Pennington gave Jefferson the benefit of doubt that the latter had not given African Americans, arguing that Jefferson had "plainly discovered to the world the adverse influence of slavery on his great mind." And in another allusion to Jefferson and the racist pseudo-science of his day, Pennington caustically observed, "he who in discussing the nature of man, can stoop to talk about monkeys, apes, and ourang outangs, offers insult to the majesty of his own nature, for which he ought to be ashamed." Black abolitionists such as William Wells Brown would also highlight the hypocrisy behind Jefferson's denigration of racial intermixture while he had a virtually incestuous relationship with his slave Sally Hemings, half sister of his deceased wife. Jefferson had also proposed the colonization of all African Americans as a way to get rid of slavery as well as black people from the American republic, a program that most black abolitionists would reject.[10] In rejecting all forms of anti-slavery severely compromised by racism, abolitionists did not embrace extremism but racial egalitarianism.

During the Constitutional Convention, anti-slavery moderates from the North and South compromised quickly on the question of human bondage. The founding document of the American republic contained protections for slavery and considerably enhanced the political power of slaveholders in the fugitive slave clause and the three-fifths clause. It delayed the prohibition of the African slave trade, which nearly all condemned as indefensible, by twenty years, fueling the expansion of Southern slavery. The new republic wrote African Americans out of American citizenship in large and petty ways, excluding black people from naturalization, immigration, and militia laws and from carrying the U.S. mail. And Congress would enact a stringent Fugitive Slave Law leading to the widespread kidnapping of northern free black people into slavery.[11] When abolitionists began their second campaign for emancipation in the 1820s and 1830s, they confronted a nation that recognized and promoted the enslavement of African Americans in law and by custom.

According to the first national census of the United States in 1790, there were around 650,000 slaves in the United States. Approximately the same number of Americans would die in the Civil War, when the number of slaves had grown to four million. It is a matter worth pondering who should be blamed for that result: the majority of American citizens and statesmen, some of whom claimed to hate slavery but who compromised with slaveholder demands, or the unknown, "little" abolitionists, who criticized the constitutional compromises over slavery and pleaded for decisive action against it. The founding moment of a republic devoted to the proposition that all men are born equal, they felt, represented a missed golden opportunity to get rid of slavery.[12] The radicalism of abolition lay in its commitment to black freedom, and it was this commitment, rather than moral rigidity, that distinguished an abolitionist from either the many apologists for slavery or those who found it easy to compromise and prevaricate when it came to black rather than white liberty.

In fact, instead of slavery withering and dying as many hoped, the United States witnessed the regional consolidation of Southern slavery, a "second slavery," in the nineteenth century. The new "slave country" of the trans-Mississippi southwest lay at the heart of slaveholders' growing political dominance of the federal government and their state governments. Anti-slavery moderation and wishful thinking were no match for the immense and growing political and economic power of the slaveholding planter class increasingly embedded in American institutions, the state, political parties, and the church. Evangelical Christianity, like white republicanism, made its compromises with slavery, and soon many Southern clergymen started defending slavery as a biblical institution sanctioned by God and the curse on Ham. The pro-slavery nature of plans to "diffuse" slavery into the west and "colonize" free and freed black people out of the country would become amply clear during the Missouri crisis of 1819–1820, when Virginian "diffusionists" made common cause with South Carolinian "positive good" theorists of slavery to demand the unrestricted expansion of slavery. As the abolitionist and political economist Daniel Raymond, a confidante of the Quaker abolitionist Benjamin Lundy, quipped, to abolish slavery by diffusing it was akin to stopping smallpox by spreading it.[13]

In the wide array of anti-slavery positions that Delbanco characterizes as abolitionist, we are left with an incoherent description of abolitionists whose only common characteristic is an extremist personality type. Colonizationists, for example, whom he correctly accuses of championing "ethnic cleansing," were certainly not abolitionists. In fact, antebellum abolition arose in opposition to the program of the American Colonization Society (1817) of colonizing free black people to Africa. African Americans from Paul Cuffe to Martin Delany championed emigration out of the country, but their program was fundamentally different from that of colonizationists, who sought to solve the problem of slavery with the removal of African Americans. Abolitionists insisted that racism, rather than the presence of black people, was the real problem. As William Lloyd Garrison wittily observed, it would be better for the health of the American republic to colonize racists rather than black Americans out of the country. He and his cohorts strove hard to convert white Americans on slavery and race through "moral suasion" in the three decades before the Civil War. Garrison not only adopted the anti-colonization program of black abolitionists but also their championship of African American citizenship in the United States, a state of affairs that most white Americans, including those who were purportedly anti-slavery, could not imagine.

In considering Delbanco's argument, it would be a useful historical exercise to explore whether those who were anti-slavery conservatives, men who apparently squashed their mild misgivings about slavery for fear of unleashing greater evil, proposed better and less painful solutions than abolitionists to the existence of human bondage in the American republic. Or as Abraham Lincoln put it in a letter to his friend Joshua Speed of Kentucky, Southerners did not realize how much Northerners "crucify their feelings" on slavery "in order to maintain their loyalty to the constitution and the Union."[14] To say that a majority of American citizens valued law and order or, in this case, the American Union and Constitution to a greater extent than black freedom is to state the obvious. But Delbanco also indiscriminately lumps together in this category moderate, anti-slavery men like Lincoln, conservative defenders of the status quo such as Daniel Webster and Lemuel Shaw, and pro-slavery doughface politicians like Franklin Pierce. Despite Lincoln's generous assessment, which reflected his own dilemma, a majority of American citizens in the North and South were either indifferent or positively hostile to the idea of black freedom and equality.

Abolitionists did not start a war against slavery; instead they recognized, as even John Locke did, that slavery lay outside the social contract, that it was an extended state of war against the slaves. This is what distinguished abolitionists from pro-slavery racists, anti-slavery moderates, and sundry Northern conservatives of all stripes, their adoption of what they called variously "the slave's cause" or the "African's cause" as their own. It is hardly a coincidence that the first issues of *The Liberator* in 1831 were devoted to an extended appreciation of David Walker's *Appeal to the Colored Citizens of the World* (1829) and a defense of Nat Turner's rebellion, in which Garrison deplored violence but justified the slave's use of it in self-defense. Slave resistance, especially the fugitive slave issue, inspired abolitionist criticism rather than vice versa. Garrisonian abolitionism was, of course, devoted to nonviolent means. The early predominantly Quaker abolitionists, all devoted pacifists, were also hardly the bomb throwers of pro-slavery imagination. In accusing nonviolent abolitionists of inciting slave rebellions, slaveholders tried to justify their complete disregard for the principles of civil liberty and representative government when it came to slavery. In fact, most of the mob violence of this time was directed systematically against abolitionists rather than instigated by them. To paraphrase Frederick Douglass from another context, pray who is the extremist here? The Kansas wars between a pro-slavery minority and a free-state emigrant majority and the crisis over the rendition of fugitive slaves in the 1850s would make a few abolitionists like John Brown adopt the idea of a violent overthrow of slavery. While white and black abolitionists, including the nonresistant Garrison, sympathized with Brown, only with the start of the Civil War would an overwhelming majority of abolitionists put abolition above their peace principles. Certainly most Northern citizens proved more willing to fight the "slave power" on behalf of white man's democracy rather than for black freedom.

In contrast, throughout the antebellum period the American Anti-Slavery Society (1833) and its many successors had advocated the immediate and unconditional ending of slavery and black citizenship. Despite what George Fredrickson dubbed the "romantic racialism" of some white abolitionists, all factions of the abolition movement would share this programmatic commitment to black political and civic equality. Historians have finally come to acknowledge what Garrison himself noted, the pioneering role of black abolitionism in the rise of immediatism. In arguing for black citizenship, abolitionists followed the lead of an overwhelming majority of African Americans and decisively rejected colonization. Championed by upper South slaveholders, prominent men such as presidents James Madison and James Monroe and the senator from Kentucky Henry Clay, and anti-slavery northern clergymen interested in Christianizing Africa, this was the moderate compromise-minded program rejected by abolitionists. Despite a few exceptions, African Americans' virtually unanimous opposition to colonization was based on unmasking the white-liberty-based-on-black-slavery formula of slaveholding republicanism, tying their cause with the reconstruction of American democracy itself. And it was one that would be widely adopted by the new abolition movement. In its early years, the colonizationist clergyman Leonard Bacon patronizingly reported, *The Liberator* enjoyed the support mostly of African Americans.[15]

It would be the combination of the black tradition of protest and Garrisonian radicalism that would give rise to what might properly be called an immediatist worldview as well as program. Unlike colonizationists, who were committed to a lily-white republic, abolitionists imagined an interracial democracy in the United States. It is a point worth repeating: what distinguished abolitionists from their opponents was not moral rigidity or religious enthusiasm but a principled commitment to black equality. Indeed, colonizationist clergymen and anti-slavery moderates in the North like the Reverends Lyman Beecher and Bacon were arguably more influenced by evangelical Christianity. The roots of abolition's radicalism, its uncompromising condemnation of slaveholding that appalled many white Americans, lay among African Americans.

Far from being naive religious reformers with no plans for a post-emancipation society, the abolitionist movement championed the idea of an interracial democracy long before the enactment of emancipation. For instance, though inspired by the British abolition campaign and the writings of the Quaker immediatist Elizabeth Heyrick, abolitionists would be critical of the implementation of West Indian emancipation, especially the long period of apprenticeship for former slaves that allowed for the resurgence of slavelike conditions. It is only after the British enacted immediate abolition in 1838 that abolitionist celebrations of August 1, the day of West India emancipation, became widespread. To critique abolitionists for lacking a constructive plan for emancipation, which usually meant compensation for slaveholders (abolitionists argued that if anyone deserved compensation it was the slaves) and a long period of apprenticeship akin to servitude to "prepare" slaves for freedom, is to miss their radical commitment to black equality.[16]

Abolitionists then critiqued not only Southern slavery but also Northern racism and laws that discriminated against African Americans. It would be this initial abolitionist championship of black citizenship that eventually made it a cornerstone of Radical Reconstruction after the Civil War. In 1865, when Garrison felt that his task was finished, Wendell Phillips and Frederick Douglass insisted that the American Anti-Slavery Society must continue to agitate for black rights. Most Radical Republicans traced their conversion on the slavery question to their encounter with the abolition movement. *The Liberator* was the first newspaper Charles Sumner ever subscribed to; Salmon Chase defended James Birney in a fugitive slave case; George Julian wrote the latter's biography; Thaddeus Stevens supported the abolition movement in the 1830s; and Owen Lovejoy, Lincoln's confidante, was the brother of abolitionist "martyr" Elijah Lovejoy, who was killed defending his press in Alton, Illinois, in 1837.[17]

It was the abolitionist advocacy of black equality as well as its interracial nature that made the respectable sort wary of the movement and incited "gentlemen of property and standing" to launch a long and systematic campaign of violent harassment against it. Colonizationist-led violence against abolitionists for advocating "racial amalgamation" and "race riots" against African Americans stripped it of its mask of anti-slavery benevolence. Abolition would gain its most influential converts, including Wendell Phillips and Gerrit Smith, as a result of marrying its aims with the freedom of speech, press, association, and the right to petition. Long before abolitionists and anti-slavery politicians like William Henry Seward evoked a "higher law" in the cause of human rights and freedom, Southern slaveholders justified interference with the federal mail and the lynching of abolitionists because of the "higher law" of "self-preservation." It would be the mobbing and stoning of abolitionists, burning of their literature, and destruction of their presses that would make anti-slavery men like Channing, who deplored Garrison's radical style and the fact that African Americans were members of the new anti-slavery societies, come over to the abolition standard. Abolitionists combined ideological and rhetorical radicalism with circumspect means and tactics: moral suasion and petitioning for abolition of the slave trade and slavery in the District of Columbia, where the federal government could act constitutionally. The first political hero of the movement was not one of their own but John Quincy Adams, who led a virtually one-man fight for abolitionists' right to petition against the Gag Rule in Congress. Abolitionists would also successfully enlist the former president to defend the Amistad slave rebels.[18]

Why did moderate anti-slavery men like Channing, Adams, and Lincoln, as well as transcendentalists like Ralph Waldo Emerson and Henry David Thoreau eventually ally themselves with abolition on principle, while Northern conservatives like Daniel Webster and Lemuel Shaw, in the opinion of most abolitionists, prostitute themselves to the slave power? Webster, whose memorable "Liberty and Union,

One and Inseparable" speech against nullification in 1830 was recited by northern school boys, defended the new Fugitive Slave Law in his March 7, 1850 speech, demanding that northern citizens actively support the enslavement of black people as the price of Union and, it bears mentioning, his presidential ambitions. Needless to say no one bothered to memorize and recite the highly forgettable Seventh of March speech. John F. Kennedy, who probably imbibed the lessons of Civil War revisionism as a young boy, included not just Webster but a senator who voted against the impeachment of President Andrew Johnson in his *Profiles in Courage*. Johnson opposed Reconstruction and once said that giving black people rights would be taking them away from whites. One must note, however, that Kennedy reevaluated his opinion of the Civil War and Reconstruction and radicals like Thaddeus Stevens after the violence at Ole Miss in 1962.[19]

Indeed, the problem with men like Webster and Shaw was a fundamental failure to imagine African Americans as fellow citizens of the republic. Shaw not only implemented the 1850 Fugitive Slave Law that made Frederick Douglass call for armed self-defense but in an important decision in 1849 ruled against the desegregation of Boston's public school system. His decision would form the only judicial precedent for *Plessy v. Ferguson* in 1896. If this was the vital center of the nineteenth century, it is hardly worth our admiration and deserves to be on the losing side of history. Compare Webster and Shaw to Sumner, who argued that the fugitive slave "bill," as he called it, violated the basic principle of Anglo-American jurisprudence, "equality before the law," and whose arguments in the Boston case would be used by the plaintiff's counsel in *Brown v. Board of Education* over 100 years later. Sumner, like most abolitionists, never compromised on his anti-slavery principles even though he differed with many of them over the advisability of supporting Grant during the 1872 presidential elections. He remained a leading voice in the struggle for black equality during Reconstruction and died fighting for his 1875 Civil Rights Bill that presciently outlawed segregation. The Supreme Court declared the law unconstitutional in 1883. Radical Reconstruction was a fruition of abolitionist ideology; its failure, a triumph of their opponents, former slaveholders, New South boosters, and their Northern allies. It is worth remembering that in this instance, "moderation" and compromise-minded politics represented by the "Compromise of 1877" resulted in the abandonment of Southern freedmen to the tender mercies of sore losers.[20] Indeed, the tawdry history of compromise in nineteenth-century America from the Missouri Compromise to the Compromises of 1850 and 1877 illustrates that compromise over slavery and civil rights always came at the expense of black lives and bodies. There was nothing moderate or statesmanlike about supporting the enslavement of African Americans before the war or turning a blind eye to the pogroms against them in the South after the war. During the presidential elections of 1860 it was not Abraham Lincoln, the anti-slavery Republican candidate, but the forgotten candidacy of John Bell on the Constitutional Union ticket that represented the middle ground of compromise between North and South.

Compare then Webster and Shaw also to Abraham Lincoln, whose evolution in anti-slavery politics in the 1850s can be charted from his support of the Fugitive Slave Law to his opposition to the Dred Scott decision, both based on the pro-slavery presumption that African Americans were chattel and noncitizens. To Lincoln's credit, as early as 1837, at the height of the Elijah Lovejoy controversy, he refused to join an overwhelming majority in the Illinois state legislature condemning abolitionists. Like many anti-slavery moderates, he accepted abolitionists' logic but criticized their methods. Before the Civil War, unlike abolitionists who wanted an immediate end to slavery, Lincoln was prepared to contemplate the "ultimate extinction of slavery" a hundred years later, in the 1950s. Compare also northern conservatives and abolitionists then with a moderate anti-slavery man like Lincoln, who after his election to the presidency refused to abandon the Republican program of the nonextension of slavery in order to save the Union but who was willing to support the original Thirteenth Amendment, an "unamendable" constitutional amendment that would have made slavery in the Southern states permanent. As abolitionists had long demanded, Lincoln would travel the road from the original to the eventual Thirteenth Amendment and from colonization to abolition and black rights during the war. One could criticize the pace of his evolution, but unlike Webster and Shaw, he landed at the right spot. Many abolitionists such as Garrison would become Lincoln's most steadfast backers. Those like Phillips and Douglass, who led a short-lived movement to replace Lincoln on the Republican ticket in 1864, would eventually come around.

The revolutionary impact of the Civil War, the slaves, who streamed into Union Army lines, and abolitionists and radicals in his own party pushed Lincoln to adopt higher anti-slavery ground. During the war, he would propose to Douglass the "John Brown plan" of spiriting slaves away to Union lines, and in his eloquent Second Inaugural Address, Lincoln adopted completely the abolitionist understanding of the meaning of the war and of the price the nation paid for it:

Fondly do we hope—fervently do we pray—that this mighty scourge of war may speedily pass away. Yet, if God will that it continue, until all the wealth piled by the bond-man's two hundred and fifty years of unrequited toil shall be sunk, and until every drop of blood drawn with the lash, shall be paid by another drawn with the sword, as was said three thousand years ago, so still it must be said "the judgments of the Lord, are true and righteous altogether."

No abolitionist could have said it better. As Douglass told Lincoln, "Mr. President, that was a sacred effort." Abolitionists such as Douglass, who were staunch critics of Lincoln's slowness to act against slavery and Lincoln's support for colonization during the first two years of the war, became ardent supporters of the president on the enactment of the Emancipation Proclamation and the enlistment of black men in the Union Army. In abandoning colonization and recommending citizenship for African American soldiers and the educated, or partial black suffrage, Lincoln had moved closer to abolitionist positions. When he recommended as much in an impromptu speech from the White House balcony on the eve of his death, his assassin, the Confederate sympathizer and actor John Wilkes Booth, was in the audience. Booth reportedly said, "That means nigger citizenship. This will be the last speech he will ever make."[21]

This was precisely the role of abolition, to destroy the national pro-slavery consensus that, as Martin Luther King Jr. famously argued in *Why We Can't Wait,* rested as much on immoral actions as the inaction and never ending gradu-alism of good men—their failure, if you will, to speak truth to power. Despite all the schisms within the abolition move-ment over tactics, politics, and ideology, it remained before and during the war a radical social movement committed to ending slavery and establishing black citizenship. Persecu-tion accentuated Garrison's philosophical radicalism, his be-lief in nonresistance, women's rights, and his critique of the church and state. It inspired others, like Birney and Smith, to go down the road of political abolitionism and yet others, like Lewis and Arthur Tappan, to revert to the beliefs and tactics of religious benevolence and moral reform that had inspired their initial anti-slavery activism. Latching onto different as-pects of and figures in the abolition movement, scholars have called it radical or reformist, religious or anti-clerical, state oriented or anarchist. However, what is commonly portrayed as the hopeless factionalism and infighting in the movement was also an indicator of its growth, vitality, and diversity. Its radicalism was reflected in the presence of women in female anti-slavery societies, as foot soldiers of the petition campaign, and, more controversially, as the move-ment's theorists and orators. In the 1840s and 1850s, a new generation of black abolitionists, many of them fugitive slaves, would remake the movement, reasserting the salience of the African American fight for equality and introducing the tactics of grassroots opposition to the unjust laws of the slaveholding republic.[22] Delbanco tends to minimize their contributions by describing them mainly in terms of indi-vidual self-fulfillment, for women gaining access to the pub-lic sphere, for fugitive slaves assuaging "survivor's guilt," a way to incorporate them in yet another anachronistic understanding of abolition as liberal white guilt.

To answer the question then of who were the abolitionists and the extent of their influence, one does have to do so
much more than bean counting. By 1838, the American
Anti-Slavery Society had over 1,000 auxiliaries with around
100,000 members, though most historians use Hammond's
estimate of 250,000. It had sent 600,000 petitions to Congress and state legislatures signed by two million abolitionists and fellow travelers, who signed on for particular objec-
tives like those supporting the abolition of slavery and the
slave trade in the District of Columbia or those opposing the
Gag Rule, the admission of new slave states like Florida, and
the annexation of Texas. Most of the signatures came from
artisans and mechanics, which belies the commonly touted
image of abolition as just a middle-class reform movement.
Many more read abolitionist and anti-slavery newspapers
such as *The Liberator, The Emancipator, The Philanthro-
pist, The National Anti Slavery Standard, The National Era,
Frederick Douglass' Paper,* and the *New York Tribune,* to
name only a few. Abolitionists, while remaining a radical
minority in the North, were at the head of a growing number of anti-slavery men and women. Many more voted for
the abolitionist Liberty Party in the 1840s and, later, for the
Free Soil and Republican parties that abandoned the abolitionist commitment to immediate emancipation and black
equality but were devoted to the nonextension of slavery.
The anti-slavery majority in the North that elected Abraham
Lincoln to the presidency was a result of decades of abolitionist agitation, which bore fruit in the sectional polarization over the expansion of slavery into the western territories. The subscription list of *The Liberator* in 1860, when
abolitionists were again under siege as disunionists, may tell
us something about the support for its Garrisonian wing, if

that, but it can tell us little of abolitionists' position as the ideological vanguard of an increasingly anti-slavery North.[23]

Their relationship to anti-slavery and Lincoln is not really comparable to the one touted by Delbanco, Reverend Jeremiah Wright's to President Obama. And though one's stomach turns at the comparison, the more apt historical analogy, only in terms of influence, comes from the opposite end of the political spectrum, the relationship of the religious right to the present-day Republican party. Delbanco indeed sees similarities between the abolitionists and the Christian right of today. Most historians are extremely wary of presentism, so it would be apt to explore what works and what does not work with this comparison. At the most superficial level, both the religious right and abolition are social movements, the former conservative and the latter radical, which appeal to Christian precepts. Even with its strongholds in New England, the "burned over" districts of upstate New York, and western Ohio, abolition, however, was never simply a reflection of religious revival. Putting aside Garrison's religious "heresies" and the "come outer" tactics of Stephen Foster and Parker Pillsbury, devout abolitionists like Theodore Dwight Weld broke with Charles Finney, who was an anti-slavery man but who put religious conversion above abolition. Garrison, to the chagrin of evangelicals and political abolitionists, would put abolition above the Bible, the Constitution, and the Union. Abolitionists, even the evangelical wing, castigated the established churches for their segregated "negro pews," for failing to speak up on slavery, and, at least the Garrisonians, for the churches' opposition to women's equality.[24]

By the 1840s, abolition, never simply a reflection of evangelical Christianity, had long outgrown the empire of religious benevolence and moral reform, sharing greater affinity with radical movements for social change like women's rights, communitarian, and utopian socialist movements than with Bible societies. While the early labor and abolition movements may have talked past each other, outstanding figures on both sides supported the cause of general emancipation and found common ideological ground. Abolitionists supported working class movements like the Chartists in Britain, the European revolutions of the 1830s and 1848, Irish repeal, and anti-imperialism in British India.[25] Their radicalism was truly transnational and challenged customary boundaries of class, race, and gender in the Western world. Abolitionism, then, was not confined to narrow religious concerns, a reading that dominates conventional historical narratives of the movement.

Evangelical Christianity would face its own battles over slavery with the split among Presbyterians between old and new lights in the 1830s and the sectional division of the Methodist and Baptist churches in the 1840s that foretold the breakup of the nation's political parties and the Union. The historical forbears of today's religious right are hardly the religiously diverse and unorthodox abolitionists but the pro-slavery Christian ideologues whose devotion to biblical literalism as the highest form of theological inquiry mirrors their beliefs. Using the Bible as a touchstone, Genovese has argued that the pro-slavery clerics "won" the religious argument over slavery. And it must be noted, the Southern Baptist Convention, that hotbed of evangelical Christianity today, apologized for defending slavery and racism as late as 1995.[26] Conversely, the religious roots of abolition lay in a broad and liberal commitment to Christian universalism, and their theology was more akin to the Christian socialism of the early twentieth century and the liberation theology of the late twentieth century. In fact, in its opposition to women's rights and devotion to religious fundamentalism, the anti-abortion movement of our times is the direct lineal ideological descendant of the pro-slavery argument rather than of abolition.

The religious roots of black abolitionism lay in African American Christianity, with its deep identification with the enslaved children of Israel and the story of Exodus. Historians have debated whether black Christianity was "revolutionary" or politically "accommodationist." But the man who saw himself as the instrument of the divine vengeance of Jehovah on behalf of his chosen people was not a black abolitionist but the one white abolitionist who shared the slaves' fondness for the Hebrew Bible and whose empathy for black people knew no bounds, John Brown. The perennially cash-strapped Brown had also published black abolitionists David Walker's and Henry Highland Garnet's call for slave resistance at personal expense, admired Toussaint Louverture and the Haitian Revolution, formed a black militia to oppose the rendition of fugitive slaves, and had fought against slaveholders in the battle for Kansas. And lest we forget, abolition, a minority vocation among whites, was always a majority conviction among African Americans. There has been much loose talk equating Brown's actions at Harpers Ferry with the modern use of terror, but Brown did not plan to slaughter innocents; he wanted to start a slave rebellion. As I have argued elsewhere, the Gandhian argument that the use of violence in even the best of causes dehumanizes its practitioners is inescapably true, but those who are confronted with violence on a daily basis rarely have the luxury to choose. And even Gandhi argued that if nonviolent protest failed to remove grave injustice and oppression, then violent opposition was better than passivity. Brown and the slaves, whose oppression he experienced so deeply as even his critics like Lincoln admitted, felt he had no choice but to wage a relentless war against slavery. Not surprisingly, when Brown was dismissed by Southern writers and historians like Robert Penn Warren and James Malin as a madman and a thief, African Americans like Du Bois lauded the white abolitionist willing to die for black freedom.[27]

Were the abolitionists then responsible for the massive carnage of the Civil War? Whether one empathizes with the war dead or the enslaved, the question of abolitionist responsibility is moot. Were the abolitionists who called for general emancipation in the early republic or the Founding Fathers who wrote specific protections for slavery in the Constitution responsible? Were the black abolitionists who refused to be stripped of their humanity and rights or those who dreamed of a white republic responsible? Were the moral suasionists or the slaveholders and their Northern allies who met abolitionists' admittedly severe words with censorship and violence responsible? Were those who asked the federal government to use its constitutional powers to divorce itself from slavery or those who wanted to convert the American citizenry into one big slave patrol responsible? Was even John Brown, who hoped he said to end slavery by shedding "little" blood but predicted on his death that a lot more blood would flow, responsible? We shy from the stark moral choices that the abolitionists presented the nation with, but we do them a disservice in not fully recognizing the stakes in their fight.

There is no such thing as a good war, as a majority of abolitionists from the early Quakers to bona fide members of the American Peace Society recognized, but some causes are worth fighting. With the start of the Civil War, most abolitionists, from Garrisonian nonresistants to political abolitionists and pacifist evangelicals, supported the Union cause and pressured Lincoln to use his war powers to abolish slavery. In the end, we can blame abolitionists for emancipation but not the war. We can even blame them for the agenda of Reconstruction but not, as Du Bois put it, its grand failure. Their detractors bear more than their share of historical responsibility for the bloodletting of the Civil War and the continuing horror of racial injustice that settled over the nation after Reconstruction.

It is interesting that the perennial hand-wringing over the deadly cost of the Civil War has seldom been posed for the revolutionary War of Independence, which established white liberty in the United States, or for World War II, which defeated Nazism. It is also worth noting that the abolitionist imagination and its reliance on the tactics of civil disobedience and moral persuasion would inspire not warmongers but radical pacifists all over the world from Leo Tolstoy and Mahatama Gandhi to Martin Luther King Jr. and Nelson Mandela. It is the reason that Barack Obama explicitly invoked the abolition movement and likened its triumph to his "improbable victory" after the Iowa primaries in 2008. Viewed from a world historical perspective, the legacy of the abolition movement has hardly been one of intolerance and war.

4

THE INVISIBILITY OF
BLACK ABOLITIONISTS

Darryl Pinckney

WHEN I WAS GROWING UP IN THE 1960S, ABOLItionists were generally thought of as white. We didn't call black freedom fighters "abolitionists." Because the inferior status of black people had been the great issue, and blacks were the dark mass of enslaved people in need of help, white people tended to think of them as some vast chorus in the American drama. White people who actively opposed slavery were the soloists and the black people who joined them on stage were illustrations of their point about the humanity of black people: that being human they deserved freedom. Whites spoke for blacks, as if blacks did not have the power to engage white slaveholders or Northern whites without mediation.[1]

Then, too, a black person was considered by definition on the side of freedom, so the feeling went, and most of the antebellum black leaders cited in an old encyclopedia on "Negro achievement"—a genre that got started before World War I—were clergymen or newspaper editors devoted to the cause. They were known by identities other than that of having been abolitionists. It would perhaps have been considered redundant. All black heroes in history had been anti-slavery.

I remember *Frederick Douglass: Slave—Fighter—Freeman* by Arna Bontemps in a Sunday school library in the early

1960s. In this biography for young readers, I would have come across the word "abolitionists" for the first time, but what I remember of the book was my confusion about the Underground Railroad. I wondered where this tunnel was and what happened to it when it got to a river.

A novelist and critic, Bontemps published, in collaboration with Langston Hughes, several literature anthologies and biographies for young readers. McCarthyism had forced them to omit the communists Paul Robeson and W. E. B. Du Bois from their *Famous Negro Americans* in 1956. Nevertheless, their volumes served a purpose at a time when most works of the black past were out of print. Douglass had never been forgotten in black America, even if white America had named more black schools after the conciliatory figure of Booker T. Washington and that of Crispus Attucks, the first patriot to fall in the Boston Massacre. However, Douglass had long been the star of Negro History Week. Black teachers loved him, because Douglass, like Richard Wright decades later, described his learning to read and write as something akin to the theft of fire.

Bontemps's biography of Douglass—which in actuality is little more than an adaptation of Douglass's first autobiography into undemanding fiction—came out in 1959, the trying but hopeful season of *Brown v. Board of Education* and victory in the Montgomery bus boycott, tempered as they were by darker events, such as the attempted assassination of Martin Luther King Jr. in Harlem. Bontemps's retelling of Douglass's quest for freedom emphasizes that the young Frederick received help from both black people and white people and that often these people were organized. Bontemps wanted to say to his young readers that the making of the man Frederick Douglass was an interracial effort, but at the same time what black writers and black intellectuals such as Bontemps—he got to the Harlem Renaissance in time to see it end and was for many years head librarian at Fisk University—most admired about Douglass was his independence of mind, his example of leadership.

Bontemps explained that William Lloyd Garrison believed that the U.S. Constitution favored slavery but that the more Douglass thought about it, the more convinced he was that the Constitution guaranteed freedom for all men. The identification of the black hero with the preservation of the Union, the connection between federal authority and the moral justice of freedom for black people, mattered in a time when the South was becoming more violent in its defiance of school integration orders. Once again, a tyranny was being imposed on the proud South, some white people said.

The contest between the federal government and state governments in the South over the implementation of laws meant to effect social change is a direct legacy of Reconstruction's defeat. In the early 1960s, most everyone was aware that the marches taking place in the South and the protests beginning up North were happening 100 years after the first promises of freedom in the Civil War. That the civil unrest was a reenactment or completion of the old crusade added to the moral certitude that helped the committed.

In *The Struggle for Equality: Abolitionists and the Negro in the Civil War and Reconstruction* (1964), James M. McPherson concluded that

> the civil rights movement of today has a greater chance of permanent success than did its counterpart in the 1860's. But whatever success the contemporary movement finally does achieve will be built partly on the

foundations laid down more than a century ago by the abolitionists. They were the first "freedom riders," and their spirit still pervades the struggle for racial justice. The victories of Martin Luther King and his followers are, in a very real sense, victories of the abolitionist crusade.[2]

Our image of the Freedom Rider in the 1960s is that of the idealistic white student from up North, but not everyone on those buses that the mobs surrounded in Alabama and Mississippi was white. That Freedom Rides were integrated was one of the things that incited mobs. We think of the voluntary nature of the commitment whites made to be Freedom Riders and, long before that, of the courage of the abolitionists, but we don't necessarily have for blacks in the nineteenth-century movement the same sense of their having chosen to join the crusade, of their having left something behind, made a decision, a sacrifice.

David Ruggles and Frederick Douglass almost couldn't do anything else, because of the matter of social inequality, and being greatly gifted, it was, they perhaps felt, their duty to place themselves in the service of their people. (Wasn't the same true for James Foreman, who organized the first Freedom Ride in 1947?) A white abolitionist in the nineteenth century faced dismissal from his or her post, expulsion from school, loss of bank credit, and social ostracism, but the black abolitionist had no status to lose. Life for free blacks in the North was precarious.

Not so long ago, I happened upon some books by Benjamin Quarles, who was for many years head of the history department at Morgan State. His first book was *Frederick Douglass* (1948). His were the sort of books from which the first black studies classes in the 1960s and 1970s were taught—books, as Robert Stepto once noted, that the teachers of these classes more than likely had grown up with. Black college libraries would have had his books back then, but so would have black churches and black homes.

Quarles's political history, *Black Abolitionists* (1969), presented known historical black figures in the setting of a broad American movement, from newspaper editor Samuel Cornish to John B. Russwurm, the first black college graduate in the United States, having been awarded his degree from Bowdoin in 1826. Quarles's study placed the forever famous, such as Harriet Tubman, alongside those who would become known later, such as the antebellum feminist and mystic Maria Stewart. Published at a time when militant separatists were arguing that events in the United States only confirmed their bleak interpretation of American history and the true motives of white people, *Black Abolitionists* sought to show the influence black people had on the character and direction of the anti-slavery movement: "The black abolitionist constituted a symbol of the struggle. Many of the Negro leaders in the crusade were former slaves, men and women who brought to the platform an experience that in its way was as eloquent, however broken the English, as the oratory of Wendell Phillips." But whites in the North as well as the South did not think of blacks as abolitionists:

In Southern thinking, the abolitionists loomed large, almost to the point of obsession. But the abolitionists whom the Southerners paraded in such constant if disorderly array were, like so much else in the land of cotton, overwhelmingly of the white hue. The white Southerner had to ignore the Negro as abolitionist wherever possible, for to do otherwise would have been to unhinge a cardinal tenet of the Southern faith—the concept of the contented slave and the impassive black.

Furthermore, the picture of the Negro as a civic-minded reformer might arouse too much interest in him as a human being, Quarles said, and white abolitionists could not resist the "ego-soothing role of exclusivity thrust upon them by the supporters of slavery."[3]

In 1817, blacks held a meeting in Philadelphia to express their opposition to the American Society for Colonizing the Free People of Color in the United States. The society's purpose was to find a suitable land for the blacks in America to emigrate to. On the platform at the meeting were clergymen such as Richard Allen, Absalom Jones, and John Gloucester, as well as James Forten, a rich sail maker and correspondent of Harriet Martineau's. The assembled free blacks vowed that they would not separate from their brethren in slavery. Colonization was exile; the United States was their home; they'd worked and died for it. "Abide in the ship, or you cannot be saved." The proposed colonization scheme unified blacks in the North. Free blacks in twenty-two cities held protest meetings in the early 1830s.

Quarles argued that colonization schemes and abolition platforms were two different schools of one goal, abolitionism. Anti-slavery sentiment had been around for as long as slavery, but the first anti-slavery society in America was formed in Philadelphia in 1775. Others were organized over the next decade in New York, New Jersey, Delaware, Maryland, Connecticut, Rhode Island, and Virginia. They were religious, conciliatory, and moderate, in Quarles's description. Their members were often men of high position; there were no women or blacks among them. In 1827, free states had 24 societies with a membership of 1,500, while the slave states had 130 anti-slavery societies with a membership of 6,625. Most early abolitionists were gradualists. Their belief was that slavery would disappear in the course of time. (By the nineteenth century, chattel slavery in the New World had been around for 300 years.) Rights of property were not to be interfered with. But after the Missouri Compromise of 1820, defenders of slavery became more aggressive in promoting the South's interests.

For what changed the anti-slavery movement, Quarles pointed to the deeds of two black men, David Walker and Nat Turner. Walker was a free black in Boston, a member of the Massachusetts General Colored Association, founded in 1826 for black self-betterment, and an agent for the New York black newspaper *Freedom's Journal.* In 1829, Walker published his *Appeal in Four Articles; Together with a Preamble, to the Coloured Citizens of the World, but in Particular, and Very Expressly, to Those of the United States of America.* Thunderous in its language, inflammatory in intent, Walker's pamphlet set out to prove that blacks in the United States suffered bondage worse than the Hebrews had ever known under heathen Pharaoh. "Remember, Americans, that we must and shall be free." Walker's tone was unprecedented, as was his contempt as a black man for what Jefferson had written about blacks in his *Notes on the State of Virginia,* for instance.

White and black seamen smuggled Walker's pamphlet into the South, its pages sewn into their clothing. Governments in the South felt so menaced by Walker's work, penalties were enacted against its distribution, including imprisonment and heavy fines. Meanwhile, Walker died under mysterious circumstances in 1830. Rumors persisted for years that he had been murdered. Nat Turner's rebellion the following year further increased white anxiety about the black people among them. Turner, believing that he had been called like Moses to free his people, led an insurrection of some seventy blacks in Virginia. They killed sixty whites from plantation to plantation. Turner's rebellion was savagely put down. Any black suspected of having aided him was executed. Slavery's supporters crushed anti-slavery activity in the South after Walker's *Appeal* and Turner's uprising. Laws were passed throughout the South making it a crime to teach black people to read. The abolition movement lost the South but gained the Negro, Quarles observed.

The New England Anti-Slavery Society was organized at the African Baptist Church in Boston in 1832; Garrison's Anti-Slavery Society drew up its Declaration of Sentiments in the Philadelphia home of a black dentist, James C. McCrummell. They were for uncompensated emancipation. If anybody deserved payment, it was the slave. Free blacks began to trust whites more because of their commitment to abolitionism. The chief difference between white and black abolitionists, in Quarles's view, was that for whites it was ideological warfare, whereas for blacks it wasn't abstract but personal. But maybe it isn't true that ideas are not personal. J. McCune Smith, a black physician and abolitionist, remembered that many people assumed that William Lloyd Garrison was black, because he was so fervent in his espousal of the anti-slavery cause. Garrison changed his mind about colonization, and black men such as James Forten backed Garrison's newspaper, *The Liberator*. In 1833, Garrison went to England to spread the gospel of freedom, paid for by blacks.

By then, new abolitionist groups had spread through New England, New York, and Pennsylvania and were, for the most part, confined to this one section of the country. These societies had women's auxiliaries, which allowed them to tap into reform movements, temperance crusades, and Methodist revivals. Blacks belonged to all-Negro societies as well as to integrated ones. The first juvenile anti-slavery societies among black children were formed in 1834. Donations from black people were important to anti-slavery societies early on, when few white men of prominence had been converted to the cause. White editors looked at blacks differently after hearing them address anti-slavery conventions. Abolitionist newspapers corrected lies about the Negro and publicized the part black people had played in the country's history.

White abolitionists such as the outspoken Angelina Grimké and her husband, Theodore Weld, who published in 1839 one of the first attempts to document the atrocities of slavery, *American Slavery as It Is,* were open about their social relationships with black people. However, most abolitionists found it necessary to deny that they were "amalgamationists," in favor of whites marrying black people. Abolitionists best loved the colored man at a distance, black abolitionist Samuel Ringgold Ward said. Emerson did not want Lowell to nominate Douglass for the Town and Country Club. McCune Smith pointed out that it was strange that social equality was not one of the stated principles of the Anti-Slavery Society.

Most of Quarles's readers in the 1960s and 1970s would have assumed that black abolitionists faced greater danger than white abolitionists. Quarles said that Garrison was not molested when he spoke, but whites sometimes waited for

Douglass with eggs and firecrackers. Henry Adams recalled that he looked for trouble whenever Garrison or Phillips spoke. A hated opinion is not always in sight, but a hated color is, Douglass said. But we now know that at least on one occasion Garrison was nearly lynched.

Black churches bore witness against slavery. Church buildings were used for meetings and became stations on the Underground Railroad. Runaways also hid among the low-down, the beginnings of the tradition in which blacks in the "sporting life" were considered more militant than respectable black people, because the former preferred to live on the margins by night rather than work for the Man by day.

Give us the facts, we will take care of the philosophy, a white abolitionist told Douglass. In his second autobiography, Douglass presents himself as an embattled intellectual. Margaret Fuller, her bonnet in Rome insulted by Hawthorne, called Douglass a specimen of the Black Race, but black abolitionists saw the freed black as a universal symbol. Daniel Payne said he was opposed to slavery not because it enslaved the black man but because it enslaved man. John Mercer Langston said the movement was designed to preserve American liberty itself.

Garrison was a pacifist, but black abolitionists like Charles Lenox Remond talked openly of it being better to die as free men than to live as slaves. Such men are now becoming more visible, thanks to contemporary scholarship. The militant blacks of the 1840s are not so far from the militant nationalists in Europe around the same time. A radical language concerned with people throwing off oppression was becoming international. My country is the world.

"To a Negro abolitionist few things could be so satisfying as helping a runaway. But the great majority of black leaders felt that there was a complimentary work to be done—one that would not only strike at slavery but would simultaneously elevate the free Negro. This was the use of political power—getting the ballot and putting it to the proper use." In 1821, a black man had to have $250 worth of property to vote in New York. Equal suffrage in New York did not pass before the Civil War. After the Kansas Nebraska Act opened new territory to slavery, "Conscience" Whigs, anti-slavery Democrats, and Free Soilers joined the new Republican Party, in preference to the Radical Abolition Party, which they saw as having no chance.[4]

However, the Fugitive Slave Act of 1850 inaugurated another kind of resistance. To rescue slaves had been primarily the concern of blacks, but the Fugitive Slave Act implicated everyone in the status of the slave. Henry David Thoreau commented at the time, "I did not know at first what ailed me. At last it occurred to me that what I had lost was a country." Melville felt deep shame when he saw a black man, John Price, taken in chains from the Boston courthouse, where the judge had ordered that he be returned to slavery. One of the black rescuers of Price who got him on a train to Canada in 1858 was Charles Langston, Langston Hughes's maternal grandfather. He was fined and sentenced to twenty days for his part in Price's escape, though the judge was impressed by his speech to the courtroom. Langston was secretary of the Ohio Anti-Slavery Society. The Fugitive Slave Law was a turning point, forcing people to take sides and sometimes to act on their beliefs.

Douglass had called for a slave uprising as early as 1849. The debate over whether to bear arms intensified after the Dred Scott decision of 1857. Blacks in Boston held a Crispus Attucks Day in protest, at which John S. Rock declared,

"Sooner or later the clash of arms will be heard in this country and the black man's services will be needed." Then came John Brown of Osawatomie. "To Brown, slavery itself was a species of warfare," Quarles noted. The day of Brown's execution, December 2, 1859, became Martyr Day in black neighborhoods. Battered Charles Sumner held the Senate in thrall for four hours eulogizing Brown, and at a time when blacks working at the White House did not want to work alongside the valet Lincoln brought with him from Illinois, because he was too dark.[5]

Abolitionists were skilled boxers, Quarles said in *Lincoln and the Negro* (1962), but in the uneasy months between Lincoln's election and his inauguration, abolitionist meetings were broken up by professionals or taken over by those determined to appease the South and halt secession. Emerson was shouted down at a Boston meeting of the American Anti-Slavery Society, and he finally sat, confused, unaccustomed to not being listened to.

As soon as the Civil War began, blacks made for Union lines. "These Negroes who had freed themselves," Quarles stated, presented a problem to the Union officers. In 1861, William Henry Johnson, a self-educated free black with abolitionist views who had attached himself to the Fourteenth New York regiment, persuaded the volunteers that "no human being in their camp could be branded a slave."[6]

Contrabands, as runaway slaves were called, swarmed the woods around Washington, D.C., while a recessive Lincoln disappointed visitor after visitor come to argue the freedmen's case. He and Senator Sumner enjoyed each other's intellectual company, but in the first year of the war, Lincoln was deliberately taking his time. "It would do no good to go faster than the country would follow," the new president told C. Edwards Lester, an abolitionist who had attended the first World's Anti-Slavery Convention in London in 1840. However, Harriet Tubman observed that God would not let Lincoln win the war until he had done the right thing.[7]

"We cannot escape history," Lincoln wrote to Congress in 1862. He was wary of reformers, but Quarles gave Lincoln most of the credit for the suppression of the foreign slave trade, and in 1862 he also established ties with Liberia and Haiti. Secession had removed Southern opposition in Congress, but Lincoln also favored colonization schemes. He dreamed of Panama, then a part of Colombia, as the place of resettlement for former bondspeople. Blacks held protest meetings in Philadelphia and New York in response. However, because of the change of mood in the country after the Fugitive Slave Law and the Dred Scott decision, colonization schemes once again attracted support, including that of able blacks such as the physician and writer Martin R. Delany, who looked among the Yoruba in Africa and the Indians in Nicaragua for a new homeland for American blacks. The blacks who favored colonization, starting over in an all-black elsewhere, were the forerunners of black separatists who in the 1960s denounced integration as an illusory goal.[8]

The social destiny of the freed black was an issue most white Americans had not brought themselves to contemplate. In *Uncle Tom's Cabin*, Harriet Beecher Stowe sends the light-skinned George and Eliza Harris on to Africa as noble missionaries after their escape from slavery, because she could not imagine these black people moving in next door to white people in Cincinnati, though she portrays them as being as upstanding as the benevolent white owners who had cared for them before they had to sell them downriver. We forget that what white people found so provocative was that Stowe made the claim that black people were naturally better Christians. Lincoln was famous for greeting and shaking hands with the black kitchen staff on his tour of hospitals and nurses' training colleges, and he was profoundly cordial to black visitors to the White House. However, Mrs. Lincoln was never asked to meet them, close though she was to her black dressmaker.

If Lincoln had a hidden abolitionist identity when he took office, he was with the gradualists and believed in compensated emancipation. Yet for all his caution, Lincoln in 1862 issued a preliminary emancipation proclamation, warning the South that if they did not surrender by January 1, 1863, he would declare the slaves in those states free. He surprised his own cabinet. "I may advance slowly, but I do not walk backwards."

Once Lincoln had signed the final edict on New Year's Day, and news of it had reached the wires and newspapers, blacks all over the nation celebrated. At Port Royal on the Sea Islands off South Carolina, whites and blacks had gathered near the camp of the First South Carolina Volunteers. As Colonel Thomas Wentworth Higginson reached for new flags for the regiment, black people began to sing "My Country, 'Tis of Thee." Higginson said it was as though the choked voice of the race had at last been unloosed.

Quarles went on to say that the effect of the Emancipation Proclamation on the black masses changed Lincoln's thinking about the war and its true causes. The proclamation was the new birth of freedom, the greatest event in the nineteenth century. Abolition, not Union, was the holy light, a change in his perception reflected in the Gettysburg Address. The proclamation also changed Lincoln's mind about arming black troops and giving them pay equal to what white soldiers received. Black delegations brought Lincoln specially bound editions of the Bible. Quarles noted that for H. Ford Douglas, a runaway who became an abolition orator before enlisting in a white unit, Company G of the Ninety-Fifth Illinois Volunteer, the war meant two things: the redemption of the Negro people and the education of Abraham Lincoln.

The Thirteenth Amendment put an end to arguments about gradual and compensated emancipation. After Congress passed the measure, a brass band went to the White House and played below Lincoln's window. But Lincoln still had mixed feelings about giving the ballot to the black man, because so many Northern states also had reservations about black suffrage. Every black abolitionist was in agreement with Frederick Douglass, and against Garrison, but not all white abolitionists were on Garrison's side. Wendell Phillips believed that universal suffrage was vital to genuine democracy.

As soon as the Civil War began, disputes among Garrisonian abolitionists broke out over the future of their antislavery societies. Garrison was in favor of disbanding, while black abolitionists like Charles Remond argued that malice against the black would exist even after slavery was gone. He, like Frederick Douglass, understood that the struggle for equality followed immediately from the struggle for liberty. "A mightier work than the abolition of slavery now looms up before the Abolitionist," Douglass said. "The work of the American Anti-Slavery Society will not have been completed until the black men of the South, and the black men of the North, shall have been admitted, fully and completely, into the body politic of America."

The split between black and white women in the women's movement in the 1970s had its antecedents in Sojourner Truth's reproach to the women's conference at Seneca Falls, New York, in 1859—"Ain't I a woman, too?" Elizabeth Cady Stanton and Susan B. Anthony were abolitionists who opposed dissolution of the American Anti-Slavery Society in 1865 on the grounds that its work was not yet done. Douglass was an outspoken champion of the vote for women. But years later, frustrated in their goal of winning suffrage for women and no longer wanting the women's cause linked with that of the black's, Anthony lashed out, noting that black brutes had the vote when middle-class white women did not.

But once the Fifteenth Amendment became a part of the U.S. Constitution in 1870, Douglass and others saw the abolitionists' work as done. The Freedmen's Bureau and the freedmen's aid societies were doing the work of Reconstruction. McPherson noted that although individual abolitionists remained active as reformers, in the labor movement, and advocating the desegregation of schools and public transport, the organizational history of abolitionism ended in 1870. Lydia Maria Child marveled in 1878 how the antislavery movement was being forgotten, how "even the terrible expenditure of blood and treasure, which followed it, is sinking into oblivion." White people in the North were sick of the "everlasting negro question" and wanted to reconcile with the South—and on the South's terms, if need be. "Peace with the old master class has been war to the Negro," Douglass said. However, a theory of conscience—civil disobedience—had influenced a government.

It did not matter that for Eric Foner, Du Bois's *Black Reconstruction* (1935) may be as antique as a work by William Dunning, even though it was one of the first studies of the period to take seriously the black point of view. Du Bois had the inspiration of looking at the blacks deserting the plantations and flowing to the Union lines as a phenomenon akin to a general strike, an action that could paralyze a nation. But Reconstruction was defeated, blacks were disenfranchised, debt peonage replaced slavery, white supremacy was restored, and Ida B. Wells would prove that lynching in the South had more to do with driving out prosperous blacks and taking over their businesses than with outrage against black rapists.

Though Reconstruction failed in most ways, the social experiment did leave behind Negro schools in the South, as Du Bois observed in *The Souls of Black Folk* (1903). "Where were these black abolitionists trained?," Du Bois asked when writing about the Talented Tenth. He called the class he expected to lead the black masses "black abolitionists" to make clear their descent from the white abolitionists who planted schools in the red clay. He was speaking for more than his era when he likened education to the mountain path to Canaan, which is probably why no one has ever called Du Bois elitist, though there is no other figure in black intellectual history who believed more in high culture.

Just as Reconstruction left behind amendments to the Constitution and an educational system in the South, including public schools for white students where there had never been any, so, too, the civil rights movement—and what some historians have called the Second Reconstruction that followed—saw new laws enacted and opportunities made available, and the movement left behind an expanded bibliography, a changed curriculum. It is hard to imagine the time when *Narrative of the Life of Frederick Douglass* and the two subsequent revisions of his autobiography supposedly did not have much value for historians as documents or respect as additions to American literature. Garrison, though, had recognized the impact slave narratives had in the North.

Yet in a wonderful work, *Patriotic Gore* (1962), Edmund Wilson did not consider a single work by a black in what he called the Battle of the Books, the debate about slavery up to the Civil War that took the form of pro-slavery and anti-slavery arguments in fiction, poetry, essay, and travelogue. Wilson made it clear that for him this was an exchange between the white South and the white North. But he went out of his way to belittle James Forten's daughter, Charlotte Forten, as an unhappy colored girl who in her *Journals* showed that she did not understand the culture she yearned for.

The first edition of *The Journals of Charlotte Forten* was published as Wilson neared the completion of his fascinating study, and maybe her inclusion reflects the impression the demonstrations and lunch counter sit-ins in the South at the time had on him. Forten left her native Philadelphia because there was no school there where she could as a black girl train to be a teacher. She enrolled in a teacher's institute in Salem, Massachusetts. Forten's poetry is conventional, but the prose she wrote for herself is alive, her descriptions of the landscape around her entirely vivid. She could get at very quickly what a flower looked like. She belonged to a reading club of blacks that discussed the novels of George Eliot and did not at all approve of *Jane Eyre*'s tone. She translated from Latin and French for her own amusement. She loved music.

Forten also attended anti-slavery lectures and in 1862 went south to the Sea Islands off South Carolina to teach the contrabands. Wilson praises Mary Chesnut for her courage in spitting on a Union officer, but Forten taught the formerly enslaved in one room, sometimes as many as 100 pupils a day. She attended the Emancipation Proclamation ceremonies presided over by Colonel Higginson and wrote rhapsodically of the day in her journal. (The edition in the *Schomburg Series of Nineteenth Century Black Women Writers* is great.) It is clear from her journal that Forten was swept away by the adventure, by the romance of her personal freedom and so much riding in the moonlight. She fell in love with Dr. Seth Rogers, and because of what was not possible between them, her journal breaks off. She had a nervous breakdown. When she took up her journal again some three decades later, she was much changed, the pious, matronly wife of a black minister of impeccable family.

Edmund Wilson said that *Uncle Tom's Cabin* was forgotten because after the Civil War nobody wanted to remember those days. But there was a second Battle of the Books around the turn of the twentieth century, when legal segregation became firmly entrenched. We know the black side of the argument from black writers such as Charles Chesnutt and, of course, Du Bois, for whom "neither soldier nor fugitive speaks with so deep a meaning as that dark human cloud that clung like remorse on the rear of those swift columns" of Union troops. But the white side of the debate has faded— the works of Southern apologists such as Thomas Nelson Page and race baiters like the Reverend Thomas Dixon Jr., not to mention the Social Darwinists of the time. We forget how ubiquitous race was as a popular subject, and the books that are not remembered anymore constitute the landfill of American literature.[9]

The rumors about Jefferson and his slave mistress appalled Mrs. Frances Trollope, but William Wells Brown wrote what was for a long time considered the first novel by an African American based on the story about Jefferson and Sally Hemings that got told on the black side of town. Brown is often considered the first black to sustain a literary career. Douglass became a diplomat and politician, while Brown tried his hand at fiction, theater, and journalism, fuming silently at Carlyle on a London bus for the insult of Carlyle's essay "On the Nigger Question."

Imprisoned on Ellis Island by the Department of Immigration in 1952, Caribbean-born historian and former Trotskyist C. L. R. James, whose history of cricket in the West Indies is still read, became unhinged and produced *Mariners, Renegades, and Castaways: The Story of Herman Melville and the World We Live In* (1953). James's desperate study interprets Ahab as the prototype of the totalitarian personality. Ahab's madness predicted the living madness of the atomic age, the incarcerated James cried. Ellison countered that whatever Melville's work was about, it was about American democracy. We are not a nation, so much as a world, Melville said in *Redburn*.

But for the longest time, American literature was taught as though untouched by race, except in the folksiness of Twain. A work's racelessness was confused with its timelessness, and for ages I had no idea that Washington Irving, Poe, Hawthorne, or Emerson had had anything to say about blacks or slavery. Once again, the picture has been filled out for me but in the context of mainstream discussion and higher education. It is a reconciliation as well as a completion of the critical task that the abolitionists of the nineteenth century could not realize: the understanding that black Americans were a part of the country's intellectual traditions.

Perhaps the most important contribution the struggle for black freedom has made to American culture has to do with the continued prestige of liberal ideas. This respect for the civil rights movement irks neoconservatives, which is why attempts to locate a black conservative tradition in slaves who declined to participate in slave rebellions or in slaves who wrote verse about their contentment are so wrongheaded. For most black people, the question of who was conservative and who progressive was determined by how slow or fast they wanted equal rights to come, how moderate or militant the tactics they were prepared to consider. It was not a matter of being opposed to equality for black people, as it was in the white conservative tradition. Even Booker T. Washington is exonerated for having advanced the cause in his own way, under difficult circumstances. For the hostile attitude a black person might harbor toward other black people, there was another language, that of the race traitor, the self-hating black.

In *The Paranoid Style in American Politics* (1965), Richard Hofstadter included "certain spokesmen for abolitionism who regarded the United States as being in the grip of a slaveholders' conspiracy" in his catalogue of movements defined by their distorted style and judgments, such as the anti-Masonic writers of the eighteenth century, the White Citizens' Councils in Hofstadter's 1960s, and the Black Muslims. His wanting to condemn both the Left and the Right may be understandable, but it isn't convincing, because there has never been parity between the Left and the Right. They don't come from the same ideas about society and human life; even the uses of religion in black liberation groups and white evangelical politics are different, simply because their social goals are permanently opposed, like their notions of Revelation.[10]

The almost cabalistic notion that American democracy can be made more perfect, generation after generation, cannot be removed from the fabric of our social thought. The past is with us, and this is not always pleasant in a country where history is often treated as an inconvenience, an obstacle to getting on with things. Yet the books march on. The status of black people has always been a measure of our social and spiritual evolution—as far as black people are concerned. The challenge for black intellectuals and black writers is to abandon the watchtowers, to give up the habit of policing the territory of African American literature and American literature, to let the new thinking in.

Because of what abolitionism stood for, and how entrenched slavery was in the world at the time, it is hard to think of any modern movements as anti-slavery's real equivalent. Whitman asked of the great Sojourner Truth, "Who are you dusky woman, so ancient hardly human / With your woolly-white and turban'd head . . . ?" For me, it would be gay liberation but not the women's movement, not the anti-abortion lobby either, even if one considered the question of when life begins and not whether a woman has control over her reproductive life. Would it be the ecology warriors, with animal liberation terrorists as the latter-day John Browns? Perhaps we are looking in the wrong place, at ourselves, forgetting the international reach of American literature and its ideas.

Perhaps it is not true that "sacred rage" may have been a hindrance to abolitionism after a while. Nothing gets started without the rebels. They are the ones who light the way for others through the illumination of their transcendent feelings. What courage was needed to oppose a system sanctioned by the Bible and seemingly confirmed by history as being permanent. That is why the abolitionists, black and white, will continue to speak down through the ages, in some place like China, which badly needs another revolution and the example of the abolitionists. Maybe somewhere a young Chinese person, a twenty-first century leader, is encountering the story of Frederick Douglass. Good news, chariot's coming, old blacks used to say.

5

ABOLITION AS MASTER CONCEPT

Wilfred M. McClay

A MONG ITS MANY OTHER EXCELLENCES, ANDREW Delbanco's "The Abolitionist Imagination" possesses qualities reminiscent of the very best features of the American studies movement in its mid-twentieth-century heyday.[1] Admittedly, there are some Americanists who would not take that characterization as a compliment. But I certainly mean it as one. Delbanco's essay avoids the pitfalls of that movement's sometimes overly unitary and monochromatic understanding of American culture—indeed, the essay itself contains a cogent critique of those very pitfalls—while recapturing what was so exciting and suggestive in the movement's earlier phases. What he has done here is to take a single powerful and central concept in the American past, abolition, and elevate it to symbolic status, using it as a vehicle for reflecting upon certain enduring characterological features of American political and moral life—and not only as an American phenomenon but as a feature of human life itself, of what Emerson might have called "Man the Heroic Reformer."

The result is, among other things, an essay that is post-revisionist in the very best way, recovering the reasons why American studies was so interesting in the first place without falling into the oversimplifications and parochialisms to which it was prone. Confident that the classic American literature of the mid-nineteenth century still has much to teach us about the American past, and that the American past in turn still has much to teach us about the present and future—and, refreshingly if somewhat riskily, that recent events may help us think differently about the past—Delbanco moves gracefully and imaginatively, across textual and contextual boundaries that tend to confine the imaginations of less intrepid and more discipline-bound scholars. What animates and justifies his zigzagging method is the high quality and consuming interest of the questions he is able to ask, and provoke, by directing our attention to the enduring place of "abolition" in American life.

In part, he is talking about "abolition" in a strictly historical way, as a particular movement at a particular time in American history, the drive to end the legal institution of slavery culminating in the adoption of the Thirteenth Amendment to the Constitution after the conclusion of the Civil War. Abolition in this view constitutes the most incontestably gold-plated example in American history of a successful radical reform, which transformed American life in fundamental ways. Whatever the halting and difficult and indirect path to that success, whatever the unintended consequences created along the way, whatever the failures of post–Civil War America to realize the full promise of a new birth of freedom—and whatever the failure of abolitionists like William Lloyd Garrison to take responsibility for difficulties both predictable and unpredictable—there was never the slightest chance after 1865 that slavery as a legal institution would ever be resurrected, or that the ultimate rightness of abolishing slavery (if not necessarily the promotion of that abolition by means of "abolitionism") would ever be seriously called into question. If this was not success, then nothing is.

In light of its benchmark-creating success, then, perhaps one is justified in talking about "abolition" in a wider and more various, even figurative, sense. The term "abolition" used in this manner becomes a synecdoche, a vivid and particular activity that also can be made to stand for the larger whole of which it is a part. In Delbanco's words, "abolition" is an "instance of a recurrent American phenomenon," in which "a determined minority" sets out to rid the world of what it regards as "a patent and entrenched evil." He does not mean to place all American reform movements under that rubric or to imply that all reforms ought to be seen as taking the same form. But he does mean to point out the existence of a certain distinctive and enduring reform temper—radical and comprehensive in its character, religious in its origins and intensity, tough and uncompromising in its manner—which seems to have been implanted in certain parts of American society, operating as a stimulative and provocative force within the larger context of American reform.

"Abolition" thus becomes a kind of master concept, a particular expression of this more general and permanent cultural dynamic at work in American society—and, for Delbanco, not only in American society but in "every millenarian dreamer who has ever longed for the fire in which sin and sinners are consumed." The dynamic derives energy from its past success but has a life of its own that continues to manifest itself in a wide variety of situations and issues, like the enduring rhizome out of whose abundant fertility fresh growths are ever proceeding. What, one may ask, does the existence of this particular tendency—a strain that one might even dub, with apologies to the historian Richard

Hofstadter, "the abolitionist style in American reform"—tell us about enduring characteristics of American culture and society? Is it one of the healthy means by which we challenge our constant tendency to fall into moral complacency and by which we renew ourselves as a culture, rather than always putting off forever the need for change? Or is it something perfervid and dangerous, rigid and inhumane, even Ahab-like, in its narrow focus and fierce, singular intensity? One of the most impressive aspects of Delbanco's essay is how it manages to be fully alive to both possibilities, while never losing its own moral center.

First, one must point out that abolition's status as master concept has a sociological implication. It bespeaks the enduring importance in the history of American reform of what Delbanco calls "the New England diaspora"—that potent offspring of Puritan faith and Unitarian-Whig conscience that flowed across the northern tier of the young nation from Massachusetts and Connecticut west into the "burned over district" of upstate New York, on through the Western Reserve and then into the prairies and plains beyond. In this respect, too, Delbanco is recovering the valid scholarly insights of an earlier generation.

There was, of course, a time when the history of early American intellectual and cultural life was the history of New England *et praeterea nihil*. Thankfully, the work of several generations of colonial historians has gone a long way toward overturning the notion that in matters of economics, politics, and social structure, New England was somehow the only important American section, the South was the deviant party, and the Middle Colonies were somewhere in . . . the middle. But when it comes to identifying the sources of serious and far-reaching reform movements, a

New England-centric view that traces the energy of American antebellum reform, as well as much other subsequent reform, back to the zeal of the Puritans still seems very plausible, and indeed probably has a lot to be said for it even today. Consider these words of Walter Russell Mead, who has described the successive descendants of the Puritans in this way: "In the nineteenth century they were the 'Conscience Whigs' who opposed Sabbath delivery of the mails, the relocation of the Cherokee Indians, and slavery. Later they supported female suffrage, Prohibition and disarmament. Today they are against torture, tobacco and trans fats."[2]

Mead's selection of causes captures the strange combination of moral grandeur and nannying coerciveness to which the Puritan-abolitionist style so often seems prone; and it also conveys the extent to which the use of the state as a positive, and often coercive, agency of moral improvement tends to be central to its implementation. Hence, it serves to remind us that not every heartfelt cause has an inarguable righteousness about it. The example of Prohibition suggests that one person's godly crusade may be another person's unwarranted invasion. Some of us feel similarly about tobacco and trans fats and other wars of choice.

This problem is perhaps accentuated by the fact that the abolitionist style, by definition, tends to emphasize overarching legal and structural change rather than a highly particular and gradual process of cultural amelioration. Its chief focus was on abolition of the *institution* of slavery and all its legal and moral supports, not the manumission and uplift of individual slaves, let alone their economic or social empowerment. This approach to reform has the advantage of being bold and comprehensive, buoyed by a sense of crystalline moral clarity. It has the deficiency of being abstract and narrow, tending toward formalism, more concerned with the category of victimhood than the conditions of actual victims, deaf to the thousand complexities of actual human circumstances, and susceptible to the prophetic urge to say, in the accents of Max Weber's ethic of ultimate ends: "Let justice be done, though the heavens fall!"[3] It is, to use the jargon of moral philosophy, apodictic and deontic rather than empirical and consequentialist.

And, speaking of the heavens falling, a consequentialist might want to point out another, more quotidian and historical, problem with exalting the abolition movement itself too much. The problem is this: it arguably did not succeed in the task to which it set itself but required a ghastly and wasting war, along with the prudential maneuverings of a president who actually was elected on an anti-abolitionist platform, to carry the day for its cause. Indeed, one could argue, and Delbanco himself allows for the possibility, that by the 1850s the movement was too divided and controversy prone to be very effective on its own account anymore, and that political provocations like the Fugitive Slave Law, the Kansas-Nebraska Act (which goaded Lincoln back into politics), and the Dred Scott decision played a far greater role in galvanizing Northern public opinion. Indeed, in this view, the chief effect of the movement's continuing visibility was in convincing the South that Northern public opinion was more heatedly abolitionist than it, in fact, was. Even the undeniably influential *Uncle Tom's Cabin*, though proceeding from the impeccably abolitionist pen of Harriet Beecher Stowe, was not a sermonic and programmatic abolitionist tract but an affecting tale of vividly rendered human beings making their way through complex circumstances. One could argue that Mrs. Stowe hit the mark so effectively not only by illuminating the humanity of the enslaved but more specifically by pulling at the sentimental heartstrings of her family-venerating readers, in depicting the appalling and pitiless family destruction wrought by the peculiar institution. It was one thing to know abstractly of such matters, another to see them enacted before one's imaginative eyes.

But even if one were to accept all these qualifying arguments, and the even harsher ones that have been leveled against the abolitionists by subsequent historians and critics, that still leaves room for one giant and undeniable fact. By clearly and firmly espousing an ethic of ultimate ends rather than an ethic of responsibility, by single-mindedly naming an evil as evil, by "reaching for the impossible," in Eric Foner's words, the abolitionists changed the terms of cultural engagement, changed the available discourse of their time, and thereby changed the scope of what was possible. In a word, they transformed their culture by tapping into its foundational religious and political convictions and relentlessly forcing an honest recognition of the culture's existing moral contradictions. *Uncle Tom's Cabin* may not have been an abolitionist tract, per se. But there would have been no *Uncle Tom's Cabin* without the abolitionist movement that inspired and energized its author and created a climate of opinion in which readers would be able, literally and figuratively, to hear her.

Even so though, Delbanco is intent upon giving the ethic of responsibility its due. The abolitionists' expansion of the culture's moral horizons would have been fruitless without the mediating prudential wisdom and statesmanship of an Abraham Lincoln. On this subject, it is hard to improve on the wise observations of Frederick Douglass, who understood that the choice between saving the Union and freeing the slaves was only a seeming choice, since "the earnest sympathy and powerful cooperation of his loyal fellow-countrymen" would be essential to success in *either* endeavor, let alone both. Unlike a Garrison, Lincoln had an overriding concern with lawfulness and constitutionality, a Captain Vere-like consistency that ran from his Lyceum Address of 1838, in which he argued that "reverence for the laws" should become the "political religion" of the nation, to his carefully crafted Emancipation Proclamation of 1862—which, one might add, has never deserved the disparaging characterization laid upon it as a mere "bill of lading," a glib view against which Allen Guelzo has argued compellingly.[4] Lincoln's moral heroism resided in his willingness to wait on the very same history that the abolitionists tried to hasten. Bound in a tense and fractious alliance, they accomplished together a goal that neither could have accomplished separately.

But the singular role played by Mrs. Stowe's novel raises another of Delbanco's interesting questions. What was the contribution, if any, of imaginative literature in the struggle to overcome slavery's curse (and what, if anything, can we learn from that literature today)? What of Kenneth Lynn's harsh but fair assessment, that so many of the classic American writers of the first half of the nineteenth century went AWOL with regard to the country's most compelling moral issue? How does one explain this? Was it sheer reticence, even cowardice? Or was there a way in which these writers were not as absent as it might seem? Is there, in fact, a particular contribution made by the literary imagination to a deeper understanding of that time, and our own?

Delbanco's answer to that final question is affirmative, and it is an answer that could be taken as a quiet vindication of the literary vocation itself, as a unique way of knowing and moral reckoning. Yes, there is something distinctive that can be gleaned from the workings of the era's literature. In a sense, the peculiar dispensation of fiction allows it to stand in the middle, between the ethic of ultimate ends and the ethic of responsibility, fully conscious of both but fully committed to neither, seeking refuge in the "negative capability" that is the special province of literature. Or to borrow Yeats's great phrase, these writers, particularly Hawthorne and Melville, made art out of lived arguments with themselves, and with their milieu.

Delbanco does not seek to exonerate them completely of Lynn's charge. But he credits them with something that the abolitionists did not, and could not, have offered: a keen presentiment of the immensely high human costs of reform, and of the horrors and mutilations and devastation that inevitably would attend the prosecution of even the most righteous cause. In Hawthorne's case, a more general awareness of the unintended consequences of morally purposive action, undergirded by an abiding sense of human frailty, served as a powerful counter to the intense and unyielding moral certainty of abolition. He understood that the same person can read William Lloyd Garrison's words ("I will be as harsh as truth, and as uncompromising as justice") and thrill to them—and then shiver at their Ahab-like rigidity and self-righteousness.[5]

Which brings us to the question of just what we, today, are to do with these grim and often fanatical "originals," as Delbanco calls the abolitionists themselves. Are they to be models for us? Or negative examples? Or something in between? And it adds to the difficulty in evaluating them that, as Delbanco rightly stresses, one cannot blink the one thing they all shared: evangelical Protestant Christian religious fervor. It is not just that they happened to have strong religious convictions. It is quite simply the case that there would have been no effective abolitionist movement without the fervent faith that drove it. Not only was there no secular abolition movement waiting in the wings in the United States at the time, but, hard as it is to grasp the fact today, such a thing would have been utterly and completely inconceivable.

No religion, no abolitionism: it is that simple. It was their religion—and to be clear, we are not talking about "religion" but about a particular understanding of the Protestant Christian faith, unique to the place and time, not Protestantism in general or Christianity in general or religion in general—that enabled them to press their cause so confidently and un-compromisingly against all odds and enabled them to say, with Garrison, that they would not retreat a single inch. This is a bitter pill to swallow for any among the reform-minded in the present day who insist upon a commitment to reasonable secularism as the prerequisite and sine qua non for constructive effort. But swallow it they must, if they are to take the right measure of the abolitionists. The expansion of moral possibility that the abolitionists wrought, and for which they are rightly praised, was stimulated *precisely* by their religious vision, religious values, and religious passion. This fact makes the abolitionists, as Delbanco admits, a very challenging benchmark for present purposes. For one thing, it strongly supports the claim by religiously based foes of abortion rights in our own day that the mantle of the abolitionists is theirs.

Combine this, however, with the curious fact, pointed out compellingly by literary scholar Roger Lundin, that none of the major American writers in the religion-soaked mid-nineteenth century was an orthodox Protestant Trinitarian Christian. Every single one of them—Hawthorne, Poe, Melville, Emerson, Thoreau, Whitman, Dickinson, and so on—was in some way broadly Christian in sensibility—how could it have been otherwise?—but at the same time highly individual, heterodox, even heretical, in his or her theological convictions.[6] It may be that the wavering uncertainties and reticences and doubts and hesitations of the literary imagination, even in the face of a pressing moral challenge, were precisely what equipped it with insights unavailable to the callow and excessively rigid theological certainties of the abolitionist style. It may that they served as an imaginative counter to abolition's zeal, just as Lincolnian politics served as a political counter. It may be, too, that their reservations about the abolitionist style loom even larger for us today than they could have in the nineteenth century and ramify in surprisingly diverse directions, ranging from foreign policy to biotechnology.

Take Hawthorne, for example. No theme in his work is more powerful for the present-day reader than his apprehensions over the human drive toward transformative mastery. Consider a story such as "The Birth-Mark," in which a scientist insists on removing from his beautiful wife's left cheek a crimson birthmark, her sole imperfection—and inadvertently kills her in the process. Or "Earth's Holocaust," in which a fire begun to rid the world of its "accumulation of worn-out trumpery" ends up consuming everything and leaving the world even worse.[7] Or "The Celestial Rail-Road," in which the hard path of Bunyan's *Pilgrim's Progress* is replaced by an easy and convenient railway, which carries its comfortable passengers straight to hell. Or "Rappaccini's Daughter," a complex allegory in which a beautiful young woman, as an experiment in the control of nature by her scientist father, has been raised on a diet of poisonous plants to make her self-sufficient—and ends up being killed by her lover when he administers an antidote to the poison.

Such stories sought to call into question the intrinsic, and potentially terrifying, limitations of human intentionality and the abyss of unknowable consequences into which our most purposeful, antiseptically scientific, acts can cast us. They do not speak directly to the question of abolition, except to the extent that they counsel against a belief in a god-like mastery of any kind, whether over other human beings or over nature. But they counsel powerfully against the kind of rock-hard certainty and overweening confidence that never hesitates to impose its will or seek to transform the world in the image of some nonnegotiable ultimate end. Such unquestioning single-mindedness may be precisely the abolitionist style's besetting fault, even as it is also that style's indispensable strength.

Yet for all of the subtle insight that Hawthorne gives us, especially insight into the overweening psychology of the "originals," I do not think we can stop there. In the end, I would contend that what we make of the "originals" in all their tangled particularity matters less than what we believe about what they finally accomplished. What matters most is what abolition itself was *about,* in the fullest sense: what it was in its essence, what its ascendancy and triumph tell us about the possibilities of America, and what pattern it laid down for the subsequent conduct of American life.

In other words, we should remember, not only the way the abolitionists pursued their ends, but what precisely those ends *were* and how the pursuit of those ends matter to us today, mutatis mutandis. How might we best define those ends, not merely as proximate goals sought and achieved during a passing period of American history, but as enduring goals, permanent fixtures in all our strivings and in the larger human prospect? Should we think of abolition as just one intermediate step in an inexorable process of radical human liberation, of the conquest of necessity itself, of the release of human potential from all forces, natural and cultural, that have constrained it in the past? Does "abolition" as a master concept aim at the kind of radically unconditioned state that Ray Kurzweil calls "the singularity" or, more modestly, at the utopian self-realization that Hawthorne hinted at in the concluding pages of *The Scarlet Letter*?[8]

Perhaps. But I would vote for something simpler and more modest, yet more sturdy, and more "negative" in Isaiah Berlin's sense, namely, abolition as a subtractive effort, the removal of a wrongful barrier that violated the underlying and universal dignity of all human beings, the same dignity Thomas Jefferson had limned in the Declaration of Independence, a dignity that no customs or conventions or social or legal institutions should be permitted to violate. Such an affirmation was nicely expressed in Lincoln's elegant if fragmentary formulation, which also serves him as a rough definition of democracy: "As I would not be a slave, so I would not be a master."

Lincoln's phrase is deceptively simple and in that way entirely characteristic of him. It firmly and emphatically rejects the peculiarly oppressive hierarchy of slave and master. But it does not seek to define the social forms that would fill in the open space left by its departure. It leaves the resultant democracy open to free development. It implies that the critique of slavery is also properly a critique of mastery, including the moral or intellectual mastery claimed by one's "betters."

Its negative formulation saves it from the charge of overbearing and prescriptive moralism, in the manner of the coercive nanny or the social-reforming zealot. Its rough egalitarianism serves as an excellent defense against precisely the certitude to which the abolitionists were so prone.

And yet, one has to admit that Lincoln's words offered no path forward to a world that might realize such a vision. It bespoke an individual preference and an identification with the oppressed—"I would not be a slave"—that were admirable. But it did not address itself to those who had no means of voicing such a preference, let alone making it effectual. The abolitionists, whatever their other faults, did so, and they valiantly and faithfully walked the path they prescribed. For that we rightly honor them. It is the great strength of Delbanco's essay to do that, too, even as it insists we show a generosity that the abolitionists lacked and remember that others also upheld worthy things. There were, for example, the Captain Veres and other honorable heroes of a "losing conservatism," who selflessly and ascetically upheld the rule of law and who therefore deserve a better name.

In achieving this balance, Delbanco's account gives us the full complexity of history, succumbing neither to the compulsion to place white hats on his subjects nor to the temptation to downplay the moral dimension inherent in this great story, one of the central episodes of America's bildungsroman. Instead, he captures a deep irony in our study of the past that the historian Herbert Butterfield well articulated: that history is "a clash of wills out of which there emerges something that probably no man ever willed," a fact that makes the study of history into something far more intricate than the rendering of godlike judgments, and the separation of the wheat from the tares. Instead, history is "a process which moves by mediations and those mediations may be provided by anything in the world—by men's sins or misapprehensions or by what we can only call fortunate conjunctures. Very strange bridges are used to make the passage from one state of things to another; we may lose sight of them in our surveys of general history, but their discovery is the glory of historical research."[9]

We get a keen sense of the role played by those bridges here, of how tortuous and unpredictable was the path to abolition, how little its actual bloody trajectory reflected the planning and intentions of any of the principal historical actors. None of them got what they hoped for, at least not in the way they had hoped for it. Here too was a lesson in the limits of mastery. In that regard, Lincoln was only being honest when he admitted, in his 1864 letter to Albert G. Hodges, that "I claim not to have controlled events, but confess plainly that events have controlled me." Indeed, as he continued, striking a note that anticipated the somber words of his great Second Inaugural, "at the end of three years struggle the nation's condition is not what either party, or any man devised, or expected. God alone can claim it."[10]

With these words, Lincoln showed that he had a rare ability to stand back from the very cause that he was prosecuting and see it with a measure of historical detachment and even irony. The best writers of the period, as Delbanco shows, could do something of the same thing. But for the abolitionists, no such detachment was possible or permissible. For them God's will was manifested not in the muddled outcome of actual events but in the purity and righteousness of their own cause and the glorious vista of a world made whole and new by their reforming efforts. They could not traffic in irony, because their cause was too all-consuming, and because in it and through it, they were working out their own salvation with fear and trembling.

One can admire such single-mindedness, be grateful for what it achieved, and acknowledge that fundamental change might never have come without it—and yet hesitate to endorse it as a master pattern for American reform. For one thing, few social causes possess the same degree of moral clarity as the abolition of slavery. And the pluralistic character of modern American society renders all such causes much more fluid and negotiable than they otherwise would be. Even if we agree with the abolitionists' judgments, we have every reason to be wary of their judgmentalism. As we would not be masters, so we would not be enslaved by our master concepts.

But all such considerations aside, there can be no gainsaying the fact that these grimly determined heroes, who pursued a righteous cause in relentless ways, left behind an example that will endure. Like them or not, emulate them or not, their prominence and their success will remain a presence for all reformers who come after them, a touchstone to which they will need to return for reasons both positive and negative. Which means that we will likely never be through considering and reconsidering them, so long as we live in a world out of joint, and there are men and women who feel born to set it right.

6

THE PRESENCE OF THE PAST

Andrew Delbanco

I FIND MYSELF IN THE PECULIAR POSITION OF AGREEING substantially with my critics while not always recognizing what I wrote in their critiques.

Let me begin with Professors Sinha and Stauffer, who, evidently provoked by their sense that I have attacked abolitionism, offer eloquent briefs in its defense. I appreciate both their candor and their civility, but my aim was neither to denigrate nor celebrate. It was to suggest that what seems in retrospect to have been a simple moral situation in antebellum America had, at least for some people of good will, its inhibiting complexities. In particular, I tried to propose some reasons why serious people of conscience could have withheld themselves from the abolitionist crusade for as long as they did. My hope was to discourage the kind of hagiography and demonology into which writing about this subject often descends.

On that score I have been obviously less than fully successful. Sinha and Stauffer want to organize the public figures of the period according to one criterion: how deeply did they feel the outrage of slavery? By this standard, slaves themselves—current, fugitive, former—will always lead the list, since the human capacity for empathy is inherently limited, and no one, with the possible exception of parents witnessing the suffering of their children, can fully grasp the depth of another's anguish or feel it as if it were their own. Next on such a list will come those who devoted their lives to bringing slavery to an end—people such as William Lloyd Garrison (whose passionate commitment, as Darryl Pinckney remarks, led some black people of his time to think he must have been black) or John Brown, whose zeal to end slavery was manifest in word and deed. Among literary artists, Melville stood higher in the hierarchy than Hawthorne. Among politicians, Lincoln's qualifications for inclusion improved as his enmity toward slavery grew ("one could criticize the pace of his evolution," as Sinha puts it) until, halfway through the Civil War, his private feelings reached conformity with what he judged to be his public responsibilities. (A quarter century earlier, as Stauffer reminds us, John Quincy Adams traveled a similar path.) As for figures such as Daniel Webster and Lemuel Shaw, who defended the Fugitive Slave Law as part of what they deemed an imperative political compromise, they were, at best, offended by, and, at worst, indifferent to, slavery—so they do not make the list at all.[1]

Writing history this way has its merits. It gives us an exemplary genealogy of people who showed foresight and courage in the past, and who can be invoked as models for right thinking and acting in the present. But it also runs the risk, I think, of turning history into a tale in which we, with our correct opinions about issues settled long ago, are the implicit heroes. Vindicated causes are easy to endorse. In such a telling there lurks a self-validating question: since the right position is obvious to us in the present, what was the matter with those who failed to embrace it in the past? Two comments by contemporary historians come to mind: Margaret MacMillan's admonition, in her recent book *Dangerous*

Games: The Uses and Abuses of History, that "history should not be written to make the present generation feel good but to remind us that human affairs are complicated," and Michael Kazin's parallel remark that historians should beware of dismissing "our subjects for failing to think and act as they *should* have—for not being as enlightened as we imagine ourselves to be."[2]

So while I admire the heat and fervor of Sinha's and Stauffer's dissents from what I wrote, I feel compelled to say that fervor can sometimes be distorting, as in Sinha's sanitized version of John Brown, who may not have planned "to slaughter innocents" at Harpers Ferry but who, a few years earlier, had led, or at least countenanced, a slaughter in Kansas. In her comments on Lincoln, Sinha fails to mention that he supported the Fugitive Slave Law well into his presidency with the same kind of reluctance I attribute to Webster and Shaw. It is true, as she says, that Lincoln eventually "landed at the right spot," but Webster and Shaw both died before the attack on Fort Sumter (in Webster's case, nearly a decade before)—so who knows where they would have landed had they lived longer? And there seems little room in the heroic narrative for the sort of sentiment expressed by a frontier abolitionist whose animus against slavery was, at least in part, an animus against nonwhites: "Every Sioux found on our soil deserves a permanent homestead six feet by two. Shoot the hyenas. Exterminate the wild beasts."[3]

On the matter of distortion, I was surprised to read some phrases from Lionel Trilling in Stauffer's opening paragraph and to find the point of view they express attributed without qualification to me. It is true that I take seriously Trilling's wariness about the motives and consequences of certain radical movements, and no doubt I share that wariness as a matter of temperament. But my discussion of Trilling (as well as of his contemporaries Arthur Schlesinger Jr. and Richard Hofstadter) was intended to contextualize and thereby shed light on the same limitations to which Stauffer calls attention. It is also my sense that Stauffer's characterization of Trilling as a sort of godfather to "neo-conservatism" is rather reductive. The left from which Trilling distanced himself in the 1930s and 1940s was the Stalinist left—not the left in the sense of any or all movements committed to the cause of social justice. Stauffer cites the scholar Michael Kimmage as an ally in casting Trilling as a proto-neoconservative; but Kimmage, with succinct subtlety, writes that Trilling "wanted to save fellow liberals from all forms of ideology, from being as unimaginative and dogmatic as Communists had been and as conservatives might yet be."[4]

Still, I think the differences I have mentioned so far amount mainly to quibbles. It seems to me that what is really at stake in the discussion represented in this little book (readers should keep in mind that it is based on an hour-long talk and four briefer responses) is the question of how abolitionism should count as part of our useable past. Was it a unique phenomenon called once to life after decades of deferrals by which the nation tried to avoid reckoning with the crime of slavery? Is it a spent force—or does it in some way continue to connect past with present and provide inspiration for building a more just future? Can we imagine equivalents in our own time of those who, as Darryl Pinckney puts it, "light the way" by "the illumination of their transcendent feelings"? On this broader and doubtless ahistorical question, Sinha and Stauffer have little to say beyond dismissing (in Sinha's case) my suggestion that the "pro-life" party of today may have some plausible, or at least sincere, claim to carrying the abolitionist standard. In his moving meditation on the discovery of abolitionism by a young black man growing up in the 1960s, Pinckney, after cautioning that "it is hard to think of any modern movements as anti-slavery's real equivalent," proposes gay liberation as its true heir.

Or should we simply drop the idea of the presence of the past? Was abolitionism a once-in-a-culture's-lifetime instance of answering the need, as Wilfred McClay puts it, for decisive action rather than waiting and waiting for a "gradual process of cultural amelioration" to take effect? Among the four respondents, only McClay addresses directly my suggestion that there may be some value in considering what might be called the afterlife of abolitionism in this respect. By titling his response "Abolition as Master Concept," he takes what is, in my essay, a kind of coda, and suggests that it might be enlarged into an approach of greater scope and reach for thinking about America. In so doing, he generously associates my effort with the founding generation of American studies scholars, who tried to identify certain essential "American" characteristics in a synoptic and sweeping way. This tradition goes back to Alexis de Tocqueville, whose name adorns the lecture I was honored to deliver and on which my essay is based. To write in such a way today is, of course, an old-fashioned thing to do, since we live in an age of well-founded suspicion about the validity of "totalizing" or "essentializing" terms, which now include the word "America" itself. I tried therefore to be cautious, though perhaps I was still rash, in suggesting that what McClay calls the "abolitionist style" may be part of a "general and permanent cultural dynamic" in American life.

My talk, and the essay that grew out of it, began as an effort to point toward these sorts of questions, and so I appreciate McClay's assessment that I managed to get some distance beyond the pro-or-con approach to abolitionism as a historical phenomenon and to "be fully alive to both possibilities"—to, that is, abolitionism as "one of the healthy means by which we challenge our constant tendency to fall into moral complacency and by which we renew ourselves as a culture, rather than always putting off forever the need for change," but also as "something perfervid and dangerous, rigid and inhumane, even Ahab-like in its narrow focus and fierce, singular intensity." I do not know if I achieved a functional balance between these alternatives, but, stated better by McClay than I stated it myself, that was what I tried to do.

"Style," then, seems to me the key word that points to the methodological and substantive differences separating the five main essays that constitute this book. "Most historians," as Sinha rightly says, "are extremely wary of presentism" and limit themselves to putting forward propositions about how and why consequential changes took place in the past. That is very hard work, and it rarely results in a congenial consensus. For better or worse, I tried to do something different: to look at, and through, a few old texts in order to glean some sense of what basic assumptions Americans shared or disputed around the time they were written and, by putting those texts beside a few more recent ones, to put some pressure on the notion of pastness itself.

In response to this effort, Sinha makes a sharp distinction between literature as a sort of complicating commentary on events, and history as a clean and clear record of what actually happened, and why. Fair enough. But history is also, I think, a record of conflicting values and sensibilities—"soft" subjects, no doubt, to which we may gain limited access through texts produced by certain sensitive observers who put their observations in literary form. Stauffer, a practitioner of American studies himself, is more open to this approach, but he says that, in turning to literature, I make "the same mistake as Trilling in confusing the relationship between art and politics." Perhaps so. There are hazards in my method at least as serious as those in the methods from which I depart.

One of them is conflating literary quality with moral rectitude. Walt Whitman, hailed today as a pioneer poet of gay self-respect, wrote some ugly things about race: "Who believes that the Whites and Blacks can ever amalgamate in America? Or who wishes it to happen? Nature has set an impassable seal against it. Besides, is not America for the Whites?"[5] Zora Neale Hurston, whom Stauffer invokes as a writer who "confronted [more] directly the problems of race and slavery" than the writers I cite, opposed the 1954 Supreme Court decision in *Brown v. Board of Education* outlawing school segregation, as did William Faulkner, whom Stauffer also commends. Yet these writers, no less than Hawthorne and Melville, have something valuable to tell us about the dilemmas they and their contemporaries faced in confronting the hideous legacy of slavery.

It should also be said that if my claims for the value of literary texts are in some respects larger than those of my critics, they are in other respects smaller. As much as I revere Melville, I must demur from Stauffer's closing comment that if "every American had been required to read *Moby-Dick* when it was published in 1851, the Civil War may have been avoided." My own sense is that if Americans had read *Moby-Dick,* even if they had agreed on its merits, they would have disagreed (as Melville's readers have done ever since) on its meaning, and history would have rolled on just as it rolled before.

Of the four responses to my talk, the most literary in its own right is Darryl Pinckney's—not surprising since it comes from a distinguished novelist. More associative than discursive, it seems to me a remarkable account of how the author himself discovered another America than the nation whose dishonesty and insouciance about the crime of slavery he had once thought complete—at least among white people. Pinckney's discovery of "the rebels," black and white, who had the "courage . . . to oppose a system sanctioned by the Bible and seemingly confirmed by history," is irrefutable testimony to the posthumous power of the abolitionists to engender hope.

I would like to make two closing observations. First, it seems worth noting that abolitionism has a high reputation today among people on both left and right. Take, for instance, the Gilder-Lehrman Institute of American History, which was founded by two philanthropists who could be fairly described as political conservatives. Yet over the past two decades, the institute has assembled an impressively "big tent" of scholars from left, right, and center—all united in the belief that the triumph of the anti-slavery movement should be taught to young Americans as the central, elevating drama of our history. Abolitionists have strong nonpartisan appeal. They were believers in what today we would call free-market values—competition, self-improvement, the independence of the individual—and they were outraged at the denial of self-fulfillment for millions of Americans. But they also believed in certain principles that we would now associate with the liberal left: collective action against entrenched interests, the superiority of centralized over local authority (except in the case of the Fugitive Slave Law), and the progressive development of law as an instrument for advancing human liberation. For these reasons—and despite Sinha's and Stauffer's point that the anti-abolitionist theme in American historiography remains alive—they seem to stand above the political differences that usually inform contending versions of the American past.

But retrospective consensus does not signify that the meaning of abolitionism can be readily assimilated into debates about issues that divide us today. Setting aside the disputed parallel with the question of abortion, should we be abolitionists, in the sense of demanding immediate state intervention, with regard to forced or severely exploited labor that supplies our own markets, terrorist regimes with whom we do business, animal cruelty, the incarceration of millions of our fellow citizens whose initial crime was to be born black or poor, the exclusion of children from health and education by a system that overwhelmingly rewards the well-born? Such a list, of course, could go on and on. If we say no to the question as applied to any of these horrors, are we sure we won't be judged by posterity to have been the trimmers and prevaricators and malingerers of our own time?

What I hoped for from my essay is that it might help to complicate our sense of what it meant to be a thoughtful citizen in nineteenth-century America, appalled or at least disturbed by slavery, aware of the limits of the sympathetic imagination, but also aware of the fragility of the republic and the likely cost of radical action. My point was to try to get away from the heroes versus villains narrative and to suggest some reasons why people of conscience, even "idealism," to use Stauffer's term for something he seems to think I distrust or dislike, tried desperately to find a middle way. He is right that some of the writers I turned to for help in articulating such a way were inexcusably insouciant about racial subjugation in America. I still believe, however, as Adam Kirsch has written about one of those writers, Lionel Trilling, that "many-mindedness is a better endowment than ardent simplicity."[6] Perhaps that is true only in art and never in politics—but I am not sure.

NOTES

1. The Abolitionist Imagination

1. Ronald G. Walters, *American Reformers, 1815–1860,* rev. ed. (New York: Hill and Wang, 1997), p. 81; Harry S. Stout, *Upon the Altar of the Nation: A Moral History of the Civil War* (New York: Viking, 2006), p. 13.

2. Lacey K. Ford, *Deliver Us from Evil: The Slavery Question in the Old South* (New York: Oxford University Press, 2009), p. 482; Horace Greeley, *Recollections of a Busy Life* (1873; rpt., New York: Chelsea House, 1983), p. 293.

3. Carl Bode, *The Anatomy of American Popular Culture, 1840–1861* (Berkeley: University of California Press, 1960), pp. 185–186.

4. Even the sternest slavemasters were known to show softness (usually short of manumission) toward children conceived with a female slave—as when the fervently pro-slavery James Henry Hammond risked his prestige by intervening on behalf of his son when it seemed the boy had been mistreated by the man to whom he had been sold as a child. See Drew Gilpin Faust, *James Henry Hammond and the Old South: A Design for Mastery* (Baton Rouge: Louisiana State University Press, 1982), p. 318.

5. William Byrd II to the Earl of Egmont (1736), quoted in Lewis P. Simpson, *The Dispossessed Garden* (Baton Rouge: Louisiana State University Press, 1983), p. 20.

6. Jefferson, *Notes on the State of Virginia* (1781), in Merrill Peterson, ed., *The Portable Thomas Jefferson* (New York: Viking,

1975), Query VIII, p. 128; Madison, quoted in Ford, *Deliver Us from Evil,* p. 75.

7. Madison, quoted in Ford, *Deliver Us from Evil,* p. 73; "ambidexter philosopher" is William Hamilton's phrase, quoted in Manisha Sinha, "Black Abolitionism: The Assault on Southern Slavery and the Struggle for Racial Equality," in *Slavery in New York,* ed. Ira Berlin and Leslie M. Harris (New York: New York Historical Society and New Press, 2005), p. 244.

8. Hinton Rowan Helper, *The Impending Crisis* (1858), in Harvey Wish, ed., *Ante-Bellum: Three Classic Works on Slavery in the Old South* (New York: Capricorn Books, 1960), pp. 166, 178, 194.

9. Walters, *American Reformers,* p. 77.

10. Martha LeBaron Goddard, quoted in Stout, *Upon the Altar of the Nation,* pp. 12–13.

11. Henry Ward Beecher, quoted in "Denunciation of Slavery," *American Educational Monthly* 1:1 (January 1864): 17.

12. Douglass, *Life and Times of Frederick Douglass* (1892; rpt., New York: Collier Books, 1962), p. 320.

13. See *Argument of Charles Sumner, Esq. Against the Constitutionality of Separate Colored Schools in the Case of Sarah C. Roberts vs. the City of Boston, Before the Supreme Court of Massachusetts, Dec. 4, 1849* (Boston, 1849).

14. For a representative sample of colonization proposals from the early to mid-nineteenth century, see William H. Pease and Jane H. Pease, *The Antislavery Argument* (Indianapolis: Bobbs-Merrill, 1965), pp. 18–59. For the idea of sending slaves to Central America, advocated by the influential Blair family, see Eric Foner, *The Fiery Trial: Abraham Lincoln and American Slavery* (New York: Norton, 2010), pp. 124–125.

15. Freud, in *Civilization and Its Discontents* (1930), trans. James Strachey (New York: Norton, 1962), p. 61.

16. W. E. B. Du Bois, *John Brown* (1909; rpt., New York: International Publishers, 1974), p. 258.

17. David Donald, *Lincoln Reconsidered: Essays on the Civil War Era* (New York: Vintage, 1961), p. 33.

18. Du Bois, in *The Oxford W. E. B. Du Bois Reader,* ed. Eric Sundquist (New York: Oxford University Press, 1996), p. 257.

19. Douglass, *My Bondage and My Freedom* (1855; rpt., New York: Dover, 1969), pp. 64, 111, 105.

20. Ibid., p. 273.

21. Garrison, in *The Liberator,* January 1, 1831.

22. Ford, *Deliver Us from Evil,* p. 485; Harriet Jacobs, *Incidents in the Life of a Slave Girl* (1861; rpt., Cambridge, MA: Harvard University Press, 1987), p. 63.

23. First Lincoln–Douglas debate, August 21, 1858, in Andrew Delbanco, ed., *The Portable Abraham Lincoln* (New York: Penguin, 2009), p. 140.

24. Garry Wills, "Two Speeches on Race," *New York Review of Books,* May 1, 2008.

25. Charles Sumner, "Freedom National; Slavery Sectional: Speech of Hon. Charles Sumner of Massachusetts, on His Motion to Repeal the Fugitive Slave Bill, in the Senate of the United States, August 26, 1852," in Sumner, *Speeches and Addresses* (Boston, 1856), p. 121; Richard Hildreth, *Despotism in America* (1854), p. 9.

26. Melville, "Ball's Bluff: A Reverie," in *Battle-Pieces and Aspects of the War* (1866).

27. Montgomery Blair, quoted in James McPherson, *The Negro's Civil War: How American Negroes Felt and Acted during the War for the Union* (New York: Vintage, 1965), p. 22.

28. William Greenleaf Eliot, *A Discourse Delivered before the Members of the "Old Guard" of St. Louis* (St. Louis, 1862), p. 19.

29. Whitman, *Specimen Days,* in Whitman, *Complete Poetry and Collected Prose,* ed. Justin Kaplan (New York: Library of America, 1982), p. 706; Higginson, *Army Life in a Black Regiment* (1870; rpt., Boston: Beacon Press, 1962), p. 29. As early as January 1862, Higginson thought that "public sentiment was moving fast" toward a policy of emancipation, and he chided James T. Fields, editor of the *Atlantic,* for being slow to get on the bandwagon. Alice Fahs, *The Imagined Civil War: Popular Literature*

of the North and South, 1861–1865 (Chapel Hill: University of North Carolina Press, 2001), p. 159.

30. Quoted in James M. McPherson, *The Struggle for Equality: Abolitionists and the Negro in the Civil War and Reconstruction* (Princeton, NJ: Princeton University Press, 1964), pp. 12, 27.

31. Letter to Horace Greeley, August 22, 1862, in Abraham Lincoln, *Speeches and Writings,* 2 vols., ed. Don E. Fehrenbacher (New York: Library of America, 1989), 2:358.

32. Annual Message to Congress, December 8, 1863, in Lincoln, *Speeches and Writings,* 2:550ff., and see David Blight, *Race and Reunion: The Civil War in American Memory* (Cambridge, MA: Harvard University Press, 2001), pp. 17–18.

33. Sumner, quoted in Gregg Crane, *Race, Citizenship, and Law in American Literature* (Cambridge: Cambridge University Press, 2002), p. 107.

34. Douglass, "Oration in Memory of Abraham Lincoln," delivered at the unveiling of the Freedmen's Monument, Lincoln Park, Washington, D.C., April 14, 1876, in Ted Widmer, ed., *American Speeches: Political Oratory from the Revolution to the Civil War* (New York: Library of America, 2006), p. 81.

35. Higginson, *Army Life,* p. 267.

36. McPherson, *The Abolitionist Legacy: From Reconstruction to the NAACP* (Princeton, NJ: Princeton University Press, 1975), p. 31.

37. Higginson, *Army Life,* p. 253.

38. Blight, *Passages to Freedom: The Underground Railroad in History and Memory* (New York: Smithsonian Books and HarperCollins, 2004), pp. 240–241.

39. William P. Leeman, "George Bancroft's Civil War: Slavery, Abraham Lincoln, and the Course of History," *New England Quarterly,* September 2008, 462–488; James Ford Rhodes, *History of the Civil War, 1861–1895* (New York: Macmillan, 1917), p. 276.

40. Chapman, *William Lloyd Garrison* (1913; 2nd ed., Boston: Atlantic Monthly Press, 1921), p. xi.

41. Thomas Bender, ed., *The Antislavery Debate: Capitalism and Abolitionism as a Problem in Historical Interpretation* (Berkeley: University of California Press, 1992), p. 9; Henrietta Lee,

letter to General David Hunter, July 20, 1864, in Matthew Page Andrews, ed., *The Women of the South in War Times* (Baltimore: Norman, Remington, 1920), p. 203.

42. Lerone Bennett, "Was Abraham Lincoln a White Supremacist?" *Ebony Magazine,* February 1968. In that influential article, Bennett answered his rhetorical question with a resounding "yes," and, three decades later, elaborated his argument in *Forced into Glory: Abraham Lincoln's White Dream* (Chicago: Johnson Publishing Company, 2000).

43. Carleton Mabee, *Black Freedom: The Nonviolent Abolitionists from 1830 through the Civil War* (New York: Macmillan, 1970).

44. See Sinha, "Black Abolitionism."

45. *The Secret Eye: The Journal of Ella Gertrude Clanton Thomas, 1848–1889,* ed. Virginia Ingraham Burr (Chapel Hill: University of North Carolina Press, 1990), entry for January 2, 1858, pp. 168–169; Gary Gallagher, *The Union War* (Cambridge, MA: Harvard University Press, 2011); Edward L. Ayres and Scott Nesbit, "Seeing Emancipation: Scale and Freedom in the American South," *The Journal of the Civil War Era* 1:1 (March, 2011): 3–24.

46. The "art of the possible" was attributed to Bismarck, the leader who consolidated the German nation-state, who was often likened to Lincoln.

47. Philip Jenkins, "Armies of God: John Brown and the American Terrorist Tradition," http://www.personal.psu.edu/faculty/j/p/jpj1/john%20brown.htm.

48. Hawthorne, *The American Notebooks,* ed. Claude M. Simpson (Columbus: Ohio State University Press, 1972), p. 10.

49. Larry Reynolds, *Devils and Rebels: The Making of Hawthorne's Damned Politics* (Ann Arbor: University of Michigan Press, 2008), p. 77.

50. Hawthorne, "The Hall of Fantasy," in *Tales and Sketches* (New York: Library of America, 1982), p. 741. "The Hall of Fantasy" was first published in the February 1843 issue of *The Pioneer,* a journal edited by James Russell Lowell. It was later revised for inclusion in *Mosses from an Old Manse* (1846).

51. Hawthorne, *The Life of Franklin Pierce* (1852), in *The Complete Works of Nathaniel Hawthorne,* 13 vols. (Boston, 1883), 12:22.

52. Edward Dicey, quoted in Randall Fuller, *From Battlefields Rising: How the Civil War Transformed American Literature* (New York: Oxford University Press, 2011), p. 165.

53. Hawthorne, *The Scarlet Letter* (1850; rpt., New York: Penguin, 1986), p. 177.

54. See Charles Capper, *Margaret Fuller: An American Romantic Life* (New York: Oxford University Press, 2007), pp. 89ff.

55. Reynolds, *Devils and Rebels,* p. 179; Hawthorne, *The Scarlet Letter,* p. 227.

56. Hawthorne, "Chiefly about War Matters," in *The Complete Works of Nathaniel Hawthorne,* vol. 12, p. 319. Melville, too, wrote a meditation on the theme of freedom deferred—a poem called "Formerly a Slave" (included in *Battle-Pieces,* 1866), composed in response to a painting he saw toward the end of the war of an emancipated former slave. He thought the light of freedom would show itself within two generations:

> The sufferance of her race is shown,
>   And retrospect of life,
> Which now too late deliverance dawns upon;
>   Yet she is not at strife.
>
> Her children's children they shall know
>   The good withheld from her;
> And so her reverie takes prophetic cheer—
>   In spirit she sees the stir
>
> Far down the depth of thousand years,
>   And marks the revel shine;
> Her dusky face is lit with sober light,
>   Sybilline, yet benign.

57. Matthiessen, *American Renaissance: Art and Expression in the Age of Emerson and Whitman* (New York: Oxford University Press, 1941), pp. 317–318.

58. *Mardi: And a Voyage Thither* (1849), in *The Writings of Herman Melville*, ed. Harrison Hayford, Hershel Parker, and G. Thomas Tanselle (Evanston, IL: Northwestern University Press, 1970), p. 534.

59. Samuel Otter, *Melville's Anatomies* (Berkeley: University of California Press, 1999), p. 72.

60. Melville, *White-Jacket, or The World in a Man-of-War* (1850; rpt., Evanston: Northwestern University Press, 1970), p. 280.

61. Carolyn L. Karcher, *Shadow over the Promised Land: Slavery, Race, and Violence in Melville's America* (Baton Rouge: Louisiana State University Press, 1980), p. 2.

62. Douglass, *Narrative of the Life of Frederick Douglass, An American Slave* (1845; rpt., Cambridge, MA: Harvard University Press, 1960), pp. 104–105.

63. Tocqueville, *Democracy in America*, ed. J. P. Mayer, trans. George Lawrence (New York: Anchor Books, 1969), p. 240.

64. Samuel J. May, *Some Recollections on Our Anti-Slavery Conflict* (1869), p. 172. Orville Dewey had served as Channing's assistant minister at the Federal Street Church in Boston.

65. Steven Marcus, Introduction to Conrad, *The Secret Agent* (New York: Barnes and Noble, 2007), p. xxxiv.

66. Horace Scudder, review of *The Bostonians,* in the *Atlantic,* June 1886.

67. Gass, "The High Brutality of Good Intentions," in *Fiction and the Figures of Life* (Boston: David R. Godine, 1979), pp. 177–190.

68. Trilling, "The Princess Casamassima," in *The Liberal Imagination* (New York: Viking, 1950), p. 85 (first published as the introduction to a 1948 reprint of James's novel); "Manners, Morals, and the Novel" (also first published in 1948), in ibid., p. 221.

69. Schlesinger, *The Vital Center* (Boston: Houghton-Mifflin, 1949), pp. 154–155.

70. Ibid., p. 10.

71. Wilson, *Patriotic Gore: Studies in the Literature of the American Civil War* (New York: Oxford University Press, 1962), pp. 91, 192; Hofstadter, *The American Political Tradition* (New York: Alfred A.Knopf, 1948), p. 145.

72. Alan Heimert ("Moby-Dick and American Political Symbolism," *American Quarterly* 15:4 [Winter 1963]: 498–534) suggests that Melville may have had Webster in mind when he described the "broad" and "snowy" brow of the hated whale.

73. On the façade of Butler Library at Columbia University, completed in 1932, Daniel Webster's name is inscribed in the stone along with the names of Hawthorne and Melville.

74. As late as 1977, when I was in graduate school, a book about classic American literature by my slightly older colleague Tim Gilmore appeared under the title *The Middle Way* (1977). It turned out to be one of the last serious books to take for granted the premises I have just sketched.

75. Lynn goes on to concede that "Bronson Alcott and Henry Thoreau protested against the Mexican War, a conflict undertaken to appease the slaveocracy's land hunger, as Lowell had done in the first series of *The Bigelow Papers* (1846); Whittier published a number of anti-slavery poems, and Longfellow followed his lead in *Poems on Slavery* (1842); but the overwhelming majority of the poets and essayists of the day did not even acknowledge the existence of the gravest moral question in the nation's history." With this rebuke, Lynn was also implicitly repudiating an earlier generation of scholars who had suppressed or understated the significance of slavery. Nearly fifty years later, Lynn's contemporary David Brion Davis, whose PhD was also from Harvard's American Civilization program, made a similar complaint. Describing Perry Miller as "the most brilliant teacher and scholar" he had known at Harvard, Davis recounts his retrospective amazement when he went back to his notes from Miller's course, and to Miller's posthumous *The Life of the Mind in America,* and found not a single mention of "slavery, antislavery, or abolition." David Brion Davis, "Re-Examining the Problem of Slavery in Western Culture," *Proceedings of the American Antiquarian Society* 118, part 2 (2008): 250.

76. Stout, *Upon the Altar of the Nation,* p. 457.

77. Goldfield, *America Aflame: How the Civil War Created a Nation* (New York: Bloomsbury, 2011), p. 16.

78. Robert V. Remini, *At the Edge of the Precipice: Henry Clay and the Compromise That Saved the Union* (New York: Basic Books, 2010), p. xii.

79. Mark A. Graber, *Dred Scott and the Problem of Constitutional Evil* (New York: Cambridge University Press, 2006), p. 14.

80. Haskell, *Objectivity Is Not Neutrality: Explanatory Schemes in History* (Baltimore: Johns Hopkins University Press, 1998), p. 256.

81. Chapman, in Edmund Wilson, ed., *The Shock of Recognition: The Development of Literature in the United States Recorded by the Men Who Made It* (New York: Doubleday, 1943), p. 627.

82. Seward, Speech in the United States Senate, March 11, 1850; Wendell Glick, ed., *The Writings of Henry David Thoreau: Reform Papers* (Princeton, NJ: Princeton University Press, 1974), p. 104. Huckabee's widely quoted statement was made on the *Morning Joe* television program on January 15, 2008 (available on YouTube). Lincoln condemned Seward's "higher law" thinking in his speech to the Scott Club of Springfield, Illinois, on August 26, 1852 (Fehrenbacher, *Lincoln*, 1:296).

83. George Fitzhugh, *Cannibals All! Or Slaves without Masters* (1857; rpt., Cambridge, MA: Harvard University Press, 1960), p. 27; the description of Lincoln is from *Standard Encyclopedia of the Alcohol Problem* (Westerville, OH, 1928), 4:1557; Brown and Bibb, in William Andrews, ed., *Slave Narratives* (New York: Library of America, 2000), pp. 388, 446; Garrison, cited in Daniel Okrent, *Last Call: The Rise and Fall of Prohibition* (New York: Scribner, 2010), p. 9; Douglass and Grizelda Hall Hobson, quoted in Okrent, *Last Call*, pp. 19, 72–73.

84. Frances Fitzgerald, *Way Out There in the Blue: Reagan, Star Wars, and the End of the Cold War* (New York: Simon and Schuster, 2000), pp. 32, 24.

85. Gregg D. Crane, *Race, Citizenship, and Law,* pp. 19–20.

86. Lincoln, "House Divided" Speech, June 16, 1858, in Fehrenbacher, *Lincoln,* 1:426.*Speeches and Writings*, I, 426.

87. Richard Land, quoted in *Baptist Press*, January 19, 2009.

88. Joan D. Hedrick, *Harriet Beecher Stowe: A Life* (New York: Oxford University Press, 1994), p. 207.

89. Christina Martin, "Twin's Pro-Life Children's Book Goes to National Educators Association Conference," http://bound4life .com/blog/2010/08/04/twin-s-pro-life-children-s-book-goes -to-national-educators-assocation-conference; Julie Doehner, Geauga County chapter president of Ohio Right to Life, quoted in *New York Times,* December 6, 2011. See Philip Jenkins, "Armies of God" (cited in note 47) for comparison of radical "pro-life"advocates with John Brown.

90. In the broad sense I have been using the term, there is, of course, nothing uniquely American about the abolitionist imagination. Every society has its abolitionist politics in one form or another, and, in fact, as David Garland shows in *Peculiar Institution: America's Death Penalty in an Age of Abolition* (Cambridge, MA: Harvard University Press, 2010), on at least one front of the abolitionist war, America lags behind other developed nations, where capital punishment has long been outlawed as a vestige of barbarity. Garland ascribes the persistence of the death penalty in the United States in part to "the populist, localistic, democratic ethos of the American polity" that encourages "vengeful passions and death demands aroused by atrocious murders"—by contrast to other Western societies where "the issue of capital punishment has been settled, once and for all, at the national center of government, not decided on a discretionary, case-by-case basis by local actors at the periphery" (p. 191). In this case, American exceptionalism—so often traced to the Christian millenarianism that has always been a strong force in American life—takes the form not of a moral crusade but of resistance to what is perceived as illegitimate constraint on the popular will.

91. In a recent *New York Times* article ("Death and Budgets," July 15, 2011), David Brooks suggests that America's broader fiscal crisis, largely driven by ever-rising health-care costs, is partly attributable to "the barely suppressed hope that someday all this spending and innovation will produce something close to immortality."

92. Alan Harrington, *The Immortalist* (New York: Random House, 1969), p. 239. The idea of radically lengthening human life may

174

be gaining a hearing among reputable scientists; see Nicholas Wade, "Quest for a Long, Long Life Gains Scientific Respect," *New York Times*, September 29, 2009.

93. David Reynolds, "Freedom's Martyr," and Tony Horwitz, "The 9/11 of 1859," *New York Times*, December 2, 2009.

94. It was feasible because "natural increase" was expected to provide plenty of slaves for decades to come. Leonard W. Levy, *Origins of the Bill of Rights* (New Haven, CT: Yale University Press, 1999), p. 253.

95. Lewis P. Simpson, *Mind and the American Civil War: A Meditation on Lost Causes* (Baton Rouge: Louisiana State University Press, 1989), p. 32; McPherson, *The Struggle for Equality,* pp. 430–431.

96. Jefferson, *Notes on the State of Virginia,* p. 187; Douglass, *My Bondage,* p. 102.

97. Eliot, letter to his mother, December 20, 1862, William Greenleaf Eliot personal papers, University Archives, Dept. of Special Collections, Washington University Libraries; Warren, *The Legacy of the Civil War: Meditations on the Centennial* (1961; rpt., New York: Vintage Books, 1964), p. 20.

98. Reynolds, *Devils & Rebels,* p. 192; Hawthorne, letter to Franklin Pierce, quoted in ibid., p. 188; Hawthorne, "Chiefly about War Matters," p. 319.

99. Chapman, "Emerson," in *Unbought Spirit: A John Jay Chapman Reader,* ed. Richard Stone (Urbana: University of Illinois Press, 1998), pp. 114–115.

2. FIGHTING THE DEVIL WITH HIS OWN FIRE

1. Joseph Yanielli, "George Thompson among the Africans: Empathy, Authority, and Insanity in the Age of Abolition," *Journal of American History* 96:4 (March 2010): 980–981.

2. On the importance of historical empathy, see David Lowenthal, *The Past Is a Foreign Country* (Cambridge: Cambridge University Press, 1985); Deborah Lynn Cunningham, "Professional Practice and Perspectives in the Teaching of Historical Empathy" (PhD diss., University of Oxford, 2003).

3. Andrew Delbanco, *William Ellery Channing: An Essay on the Liberal Spirit in America* (Cambridge, MA: Harvard University Press, 1981); Anne-Marie Taylor, *Young Charles Sumner and the Legacy of the American Enlightenment* (Amherst: University of Massachusetts Press, 2001), pp. 137–146.

4. David Brion Davis, *The Problem of Slavery in Western Culture* (1966; rpt., New York: Oxford University Press, 1988), pp. 291–332; Davis, *The Problem of Slavery in the Age of Revolution, 1770–1823* (Ithaca, NY: Cornell University Press, 1975), chs. 4–5; Ryan P. Jordan, *Slavery and the Meetinghouse: The Quakers and the Abolitionist Dilemma, 1820–1865* (Bloomington: Indiana University Press, 2007); Jean R. Soderlund, *Quakers and Slavery: A Divided Spirit* (Princeton, NJ: Princeton University Press, 1985); Hiram H. Hilty, *Toward Freedom for All: North Carolina Quakers and Slavery* (Richmond, IN: Friends United Press, 1984); Gary B. Nash, *Quakers and Politics: Pennsylvania, 1681–1726* (Princeton, NJ: Princeton University Press, 1968).

5. Delbanco himself comes close to acknowledging that the liberal aesthetic he champions is a largely white one when he refers to his liberal writers' comparative silence on slavery: "I do not think it is *quite right* to say that antebellum writers stayed silent about slavery, but when they did approach the subject, they—even Melville—did so obliquely" (emphasis added).

6. At times Delbanco seems to imply that Frederick Douglass and Martin Luther King Jr. are among his pantheon of liberals and centrists. In fact, Douglass and King hated liberals for their "go slow" approach to reform. Both men championed immediatism and vigorously opposed the ethos of gradual reform that is central to Delbanco's liberal aesthetic. Delbanco's statement that an abolitionist wants to eradicate a "heinous evil"—"not tomorrow, not next year, but now" perfectly captures Douglass's and King's worldview.

7. In 1842 Longfellow published a book of anti-slavery poetry, *Poems on Slavery* (1842).

8. Hawthorne to H. L. Longfellow, May 8, 1851, quoted in *The Centenary Edition of the Works of Nathaniel Hawthorne,* vol.

16: *The Letters, 1843–1853,* ed. Thomas Woodson, L. Neal Smith, and Norman Holmes Pearson (Columbus: Ohio State University Press, 1985), pp. 430–431.

9. Fanny Longfellow to Charles Sumner, May 14, 1851, Charles Sumner Papers, Houghton Library, Harvard University, quoted in a copy at the Henry Wadsworth Longfellow House Archives, Box 87, Folder 7: "Sumner, Charles. Research."

10. Hawthorne to Bridge, April 1, 1844, quoted in *Works of Hawthorne,* vol. 16, p. 26.

11. Acts 10:34.

12. Nathaniel Hawthorne, *Life of Franklin Pierce* (1852; rpt., Honolulu: University Press of the Pacific, 2002), p. 90 (emphasis added); Hawthorne to Bridge, October 18, 1852, quoted in Patrick Brancaccio, "'The Black Man's Paradise': Hawthorne's Editing of the Journal of an African Cruiser," *New England Quarterly* 53:1 (March 1980): 33n27.

13. Larry Gara, *The Presidency of Franklin Pierce* (Lawrence: University Press of Kansas, 1991), p. xi; Hawthorne to Bridge, October 12, 1861, quoted in *The Centenary Edition of the Works of Nathaniel Hawthorne,* vol. 18: *The Letters, 1857–1864,* ed. Thomas Woodson, James A. Rubino, L. Neal Smith, and Norman Holmes Pearson (Columbus: Ohio State University Press, 1987), p. 412.

   For additional references to Hawthorne's Copperhead views, particularly his desire for the dissolution of the Union and a separate slaveholding nation, see Hawthorne to William D. Ticknor, February 10, 1860, in *Works of Hawthorne,* vol. 18, p. 226; Hawthorne to Henry A. Bright, November 14, 1861, in ibid., pp. 420–422; Hawthorne to Elizabeth Peabody, July 20, 1863, in ibid., pp. 589–594.

14. Jennifer L. Weber, *Copperheads: The Rise and Fall of Lincoln's Opponents in the North* (New York: Oxford University Press, 2006), pp. 98–100, 124–129, 209; Robert Churchill, "The Sons of Liberty Conspiracy, 1863–1864," *Prologue* 30 (1998): 295–302; Wood Gray, *The Hidden Civil War: The Story of the Copperheads* (New York: Viking Press, 1942), pp. 183–206; Robert Douthat Meade, *Judah P. Benjamin, Confederate Statesman*

(1943; rpt., Baton Rouge: Louisiana State University Press), p. 298 (quoted). According to Meade, "there is no proof that the Confederate agents in Canada or the North actually attempted to contact Pierce."

15. Hawthorne to Franklin Pierce, July 24, 1863, in *Works of Hawthorne,* vol. 18, p. 595. Hawthorne requested Davis's autograph from Pierce, a friend of Davis. The best defense of Hawthorne's politics is Larry J. Reynolds, *Devils and Rebels: The Making of Hawthorne's Damned Politics* (Ann Arbor: University of Michigan Press, 2008). Reynolds makes a case for Hawthorne's concerns over slavery, but at the same time he acknowledges Hawthorne's lack of sympathy toward blacks. He also characterizes Hawthorne as a pacifist, which I find unconvincing because it required Hawthorne to ignore that fact that violence was the bolt around which slavery depended.

16. Henry James, *Notes of a Son and Brother,* in *Autobiography,* ed. Frederick W. Dupee (New York: Criterion Books, 1956), p. 457; Kenneth W. Warren, *Black and White Strangers: Race and American Literary Realism* (Chicago: University of Chicago Press, 1993), p. 19.

17. Henry James, *William Whetmore Story and His Friends: From Letters, Diaries, and Recollections,* 2 vols. (Boston: Houghton, Mifflin & Co., 1903), quotations from vol. 1, pp. 84, 234, and vol. 2, pp. 29, 30, 31, 160.

18. George M. Fredrickson, *The Inner Civil War: Northern Intellectuals and the Crisis of the Union* (1965; rpt., Urbana: University of Illinois Press, 1993), ch. 12; Louis Menand, *The Metaphysical Club: A Story of Ideas in America* (New York: Farrar, Straus and Giroux, 2001), pp. 337–376.

19. Warren, *Black and White Strangers,* pp. 18–21, quotation from p. 20; Henry James, "American Letters," April 23, 1898, in *Henry James: Literary Criticism* (New York: Library of America, 1984), 1:665, 666.

20. Henry James, *The American Scene* (1907; rpt., New York: Penguin Books, 1994), pp. 276, 307; Warren, *Black and White Strangers,* p. 116.

21. Warren, *Black and White Strangers*, p. 22, 115, 120, quotation from p. 22. Sara Blair elaborates on some of the themes raised by Warren; see Sara Blair, *Henry James and the Writing of Race and Nation* (Cambridge: Cambridge University Press, 1996). See also Alan Trachtenberg's brilliant critique of *The American Scene* in *Shades of Hiawatha: Staging Indians, Making Americans, 1880–1930* (New York: Hill and Wang, 2004), pp. 98–139; and Blair, *Henry James*. For a counterpoint to Warren and Blair, see Ross Posnock, "Affirming the Alien: The Pragmatist Pluralism of *The American Scene*," in *The Cambridge Companion to Henry James*, ed. Jonathan Freedman (Cambridge: Cambridge University Press, 1998), pp. 224–246; and Posnock, *The Trial of Curiosity: Henry James, William James, and the Challenge of Modernity* (New York: Oxford University Press, 1991), ch. 6. Warren, Blair, and Posnock debate James's treatment of race in *The American Scene* in *The Henry James Review* 16:3 (Fall 1995): 264–285.

22. Harvey Teres, "Lionel Trilling," in *The Cambridge History of Literary Criticism*, vol. 7: *Modernism and the New Criticism*, ed. A. Walton Litz, Louis Menand, and Lawrence Rainey (Cambridge: Cambridge University Press, 2000), pp. 423–438, quotation from p. 436.

23. Michael Kimmage, *The Conservative Turn: Lionel Trilling, Whittaker Chambers, and the Lessons of Anti-Communism* (Cambridge, MA: Harvard University Press, 2009), pp. 1–14, 173–202, 236–267, quotations from pp. 7, 9, 12.

    Cornel West reaches a similar conclusion as Kimmage, though his essay lacks the rich intellectual, literary, and cultural currents that Kimmage develops in his dual biography of Trilling and Chambers. West calls Trilling "the godfather of the contemporary neo-conservatives." See Cornel West, "Lionel Trilling: Godfather of Neo-Conservatism," *New Politics* (Summer 1986), reprinted in *Lionel Trilling and the Critics: Opposing Selves,* ed. John Rodden (Lincoln: University of Nebraska Press, 1999), pp. 395–403, quotation from p. 395. See also Michael E. Nowlin, "Lionel Trilling and the Institutionalization of Humanism," *Journal of American Studies* 25:1 (April 1991): 23–38.

24. Joseph Frank, "Lionel Trilling and the Conservative Imagination," *Sewanee Review* (Spring 1956), reprinted in Rodden, *Lionel Trilling and the Critics,* pp. 223–237, quotation from p. 227.

25. Frank, "Lionel Trilling and the Conservative Imagination," p. 227. Throughout Frank's multivolume and award-winning biography of Dostoevsky, he brilliantly maintains a dialectical tension between Dostoevsky's art and politics. See Frank, *Dostoevsky,* 5 vols. (Princeton, NJ: Princeton University Press, 1976–2002).

    Delbanco assesses the politics of Hawthorne, James, and Trilling by analyzing their art and criticism. As should be clear, I reach a different understanding of these men's political views by analyzing their letters and overt political writings.

26. David Brion Davis, *Inhuman Bondage: The Rise and Fall of Slavery in the New World* (New York: Oxford University Press, 2006), pp. 153, 155; Lamont D. Thomas, *Rise to Be a People: A Biography of Paul Cuffe* (Urbana: University of Illinois Press, 1986); Julie Winch, *A Gentleman of Color: The Life of James Forten* (New York: Oxford University Press, 2002); and John Stauffer, "In the Shadow of a Dream: White Abolitionists and Race." presented at the Fifth Annual Gilder Lehrman Center International Conference, November 2003, http://www.yale.edu/glc/events/race/Stauffer.pdf.

27. James Madison, quoted in Matthew T. Mellon, *Early American Views on Negro Slavery* (Boston: Meador Publishing, 1934), p. 158; Davis, *Inhuman Bondage,* pp. 141–156; Davis, *Problem of Slavery in the Age of Revolution,* pp. 255–284; Gary B. Nash, *Race and Revolution* (Madison, WI: Madison House, 1990), pp. 25–56, 151–158; Robert Pierce Forbes, *The Missouri Compromise and Its Aftermath: Slavery and the Meaning of America* (Chapel Hill: University of North Carolina Press, 2007), pp. 1–68; Matthew Mason, *Slavery and Politics in the Early Republic* (Chapel Hill: University of North Carolina Press, 2008), pp. 1–129.

28. Davis, *Problem of Slavery in the Age of Revolution,* pp. 255–284; Laurent Dubois, *A Colony of Citizens: Revolution and Slave Emancipation in the French Caribbean, 1787–1804* (Chapel Hill: University of North Carolina Press, 2004), pp. 28–29,

162–168; James Oliver Horton and Lois E. Horton, *Slavery and the Making of America* (New York: Oxford University Press, 2004), pp. 50–51.

29. John R. Thomas, "Romantic Reform in America, 1815–1865," *American Quarterly* 17:4 (Winter 1965): 656–681; Richard S. Newman, *Transformation of American Abolition: Fighting Slavery in the Early Republic* (Chapel Hill: University of North Carolina Press, 2001), pp. 1–85; Newman, *Freedom's Prophet: Bishop Richard Allen, the AME Church, and the Black Founding Fathers* (New York: New York University Press, 2008), pp. 1–157; Winch, *Gentleman of Color;* Timothy Patrick McCarthy and John Stauffer, eds., *Prophets of Protest: Reconsidering the History of American Abolitionism* (New York: New Press, 2006, introduction; and Stauffer, "Abolition and Antislavery," in *The Oxford Handbook of Slavery in the Americas,* ed. Robert Paquette and Mark M. Smith (New York: Oxford University Press, 2010), pp. 559–563.

30. Paul Finkelman, *Slavery and the Founders: Race and Liberty in the Age of Jefferson* (Armonk, NY: M. E. Sharpe, 1996), p. 100 (quoted); Davis, *Problem of Slavery in the Age of Revolution,* pp. 119–136, 306–342; Stauffer, "Abolition and Antislavery," pp. 559–563; Garry Wills, *"Negro President": Jefferson and the Slave Power* (New York: Houghton Mifflin, 2003).

31. Davis, *Inhuman Bondage,* p. 156; Arthur Zilversmit, *The First Emancipation: The Abolition of Slavery in the North* (Chicago: University of Chicago Press, 1967); Stauffer, "Abolition and Antislavery," pp. 559–563; Orlando Patterson, *Slavery and Social Death: A Comparative Study* (Cambridge, MA: Harvard University Press, 1982), pp. 159–171; Gordon Wood, *Empire of Liberty: A History of the Early Republic, 1789–1815* (New York: Oxford University Press, 2009), pp. 508–542.

The Revolutionary War resulted in more slaves being freed than at any time until the Civil War, but freedom stemmed more from military exigencies than from any ideological opposition to slavery. Between 15,000 and 20,000 slaves of Patriot masters joined the British forces, and about 5,000 slaves served as Patriots, a majority of them receiving their freedom. See Stauffer, "Abolition and Antislavery," p. 561.

32. Forbes, *The Missouri Compromise,* pp. 1–32; David Brion Davis, *Challenging the Boundaries of Slavery* (Cambridge, MA: Harvard University Press, 2003), ch. 2; David Brion Davis, "Expanding the Republic, 1820–1860," in Bernard Bailyn, Robert Dallek, David Brion Davis, David Herbert Donald, and John L. Thomas, *The Great Republic: A History of the American People,* 4th ed. (Lexington, MA: D. C. Heath, 1992), pp. 488–491; Wood, *Empire of Liberty,* pp. 508–542.

33. David Brion Davis, *Slavery and Human Progress* (New York: Oxford University Press, 1984), p. 168.

34. Stauffer, "Abolition and Antislavery," p. 563; McCarthy and Stauffer, *Prophets of Protest,* introduction; Richard S. Newman, Patrick Rael, and Phillip Lapsansky, eds., *Pamphlets of Protest: An Anthology of Early African-American Protest Literature, 1790–1860* (New York: Routledge, 2000), pp. 1–83.

35. The St. Domingue Revolution, which culminated with Haiti becoming a free black republic in 1804, horrified Southerners. Emancipation in Haiti was only the beginning of New World and European emancipation movements. In 1807 Prussia and Poland emancipated their serfs; in 1813–1814 Argentina and Colombia inaugurated gradual emancipation; from 1816 to 1819 the Baltic provinces of Russia's empire ended serfdom; Central American colonies began emancipating slaves in 1823; England emancipated slaves in its West Indies territory in 1834; and in 1848 slavery and serfdom were abolished in the German states, the Austrian empire, and the French and Danish West Indies.

See Edward Bartlett Rugemer, *The Problem of Emancipation: The Caribbean Roots of the American Civil War* (Baton Rouge: Louisiana State University Press, 2008); Matthew J. Clavin, *Toussaint Louverture and the American Civil War: The Promise and Peril of a Second Haitian Revolution* (Philadelphia: University of Pennsylvania Press, 2009); Peter Kolchin, *Unfree Labor: American Slavery and Russian Serfdom* (Cambridge, MA: Harvard University Press, 1987), p. 49; Robert William Fogel and Stanley L.

Engerman, *Time on the Cross: The Economics of American Negro Slavery* (Boston: Little, Brown, 1974), pp. 29–38; and Jerome Blum, *The End of the Old Order in Rural Europe* (Princeton, NJ: Princeton University Press, 1978), parts 2–3.

36. Forbes, *Missouri Compromise,* pp. 69–120; Davis, *Challenging the Boundaries,* ch. 2; Stauffer, "Missouri Compromise," in *A New Literary History of America,* ed. Greil Marcus and Werner Sollors (Cambridge, MA: Harvard University Press, 2009), pp. 150–154.

37. Davis, *Challenging the Boundaries,* pp. 35–59, quotation by Rufus King from pp. 41–42; Forbes, *Missouri Compromise,* pp. 141–209.

38. Davis, *Challenging the Boundaries,* pp. 35–59; Forbes, *Missouri Compromise,* pp. 141–209; Stauffer, "Missouri Compromise," pp. 150–154; James Brewer Stewart, *Holy Warriors: The Abolitionists and American Slavery,* rev. ed. (New York: Hill and Wang, 1997), pp. 3–50.

39. Stewart, *Holy Warriors,* chs. 2–7; Davis, *Inhuman Bondage,* pp. 250–267; John Stauffer, *The Black Hearts of Men: Radical Abolitionists and the Transformation of Race* (Cambridge, MA: Harvard University Press, 2002), pp. 134–144; William Lee Miller, *Arguing about Slavery: John Quincy Adams and the Great Battle in the United States Congress* (New York: Vintage Press, 1998); Betty L. Fladeland, "Compensated Emancipation: A Rejected Alternative," *Journal of Southern History* 42:4 (May 1976): 169–186. On Douglass and Melville both using "slumbering volcano," see John W. Blassingame, ed., *The Frederick Douglass Papers,* ser. 1, vol. 2 (New Haven, CT: Yale University Press, 1982), p. 151; Melville, *Bartleby and Benito Cereno* (New York: Dover Publications, 1990), p. 58.

40. Davis, *Challenging the Boundaries,* ch. 2; Stauffer, "Missouri Compromise," pp. 150–154.

41. Stewart, *Holy Warriors,* pp. 11–50; Davis, *Inhuman Bondage,* pp. 250–267; Stauffer, *Black Hearts of Men,* pp. 95–110.

42. Stewart, *Holy Warriors,* pp. 127–150; Stauffer, "In the Shadow of a Dream"; Stauffer, *Black Hearts of Men,* chs. 1, 5.

43. Manisha Sinha, *The Counterrevolution of Slavery: Politics and Ideology in Antebellum South Carolina* (Chapel Hill: University of North Carolina Press, 2000); Davis, *Inhuman Bondage,* pp. 175–192, 268–296; William W. Freehling, *The Road to Disunion: Secessionists at Bay, 1776–1854* (New York: Oxford University Press, 1990), parts 5–7; Clement Eaton, *Freedom-of-Thought Struggle in the Old South,* rev. ed. (New York: Harper and Row, 1964); Miller, *Arguing about Slavery,* pp. 79–105; James W. Silver, "Mississippi: The Closed Society," *Journal of Southern History* 30:1 (February 1964): 3–4.

44. Henry Wilson, *History of the Rise and Fall of the Slave Power in America,* vol. 1 (Boston: Houghton Mifflin, 1872), pp. 429–430, 671, quotations from pp. 429, 671; Wilson, *History of the Rise and Fall of the Slave Power in America,* vol. 2, p. 162 (quoted); Miller, *Arguing about Slavery,* pp. 208–209, 216, 354–355, 440–452, 508.

45. Paul Finkelman, *An Imperfect Union: Slavery, Federalism, and Comity* (Chapel Hill: University of North Carolina Press, 1981), pp. 285–344; Paul M. Angle, ed., *Created Equal? The Complete Lincoln-Douglas Debates of 1858* (Chicago: University of Chicago Press, 1958), pp. 309–311, 328–329, 337–338, 377–378; John Stauffer, *Giants: The Parallel Lives of Frederick Douglass and Abraham Lincoln* (New York: Twelve, 2008), pp. 194–198.

46. Angle, *Created Equal?,* pp. 2, 270; Seymour Drescher, *Abolition: A History of Slavery and Antislavery* (Cambridge: Cambridge University Press, 2009), pp. 294–332. For other statesmen who predicted that a gradual end to slavery would require a century or more, see St. George Tucker, in Nash, *Race and Revolution,* pp. 154–158; and James Madison, in Louis Ruchames, ed., *Racial Thought in America: A Documentary History,* vol. 1 (Amherst: University of Massachusetts Press, 1969), pp. 283–287. Although Henry Clay never gives a specific time frame, he implies that gradual abolition will take at least a century. See Robert V. Remini, *Henry Clay: Statesman for the Union* (New York: W. W. Norton, 1991), pp. 484, 526, 618, 718.

47. The new Thirteenth Amendment opens with the following words: "No amendment shall be made to the Constitution which will authorize or give to Congress the power to abolish or interfere, within any State, with the domestic institutions thereof, including that of persons held to labor or service by the laws of said State." See Stauffer, *Giants,* pp. 215–219, 255–257; William M. Wiecek, *The Sources of Antislavery Constitutionalism in America, 1760–1848* (Ithaca, NY: Cornell University Press, 1977), pp. 276–287.

48. Abraham Lincoln, *Great Speeches* (New York: Dover Publications, 1991), p. 59.

49. David M. Oshinsky, *Worse than Slavery: Parchman Farm and the Ordeal of Jim Crow Justice* (New York: Free Press, 1997); Douglas A. Blackmon, *Slavery by Another Name: The Reenslavement of Black Americans from the Civil War to World War II* (New York: Anchor Books, 2009); Leon F. Litwack, *Trouble in Mind: Black Southerners in the Age of Jim Crow* (New York: Vintage Books, 1999).

50. Tourgee, quoted in Stephen Budiansky, *The Bloody Shirt: Terror after Appomattox* (New York: Viking, 2008), p. 9.

51. David W. Blight, *Race and Reunion: The Civil War in American Memory* (Cambridge, MA: Harvard University Press, 2001), pp. 1–139.

    Charles Sumner was among the few who understood Southern rage and honor, having experienced its effects firsthand. He wanted Confederate leaders to be sent "into exile," but his plea fell on deaf ears. David Herbert Donald, *Charles Sumner: Part II: Charles Sumner and the Rights of Man* (1970; rpt., New York: Da Capo, 1996), p. 221.

52. Stauffer, *Black Hearts of Men,* p. 207; Litwack, *Trouble in Mind;* Oshinsky, *Worse than Slavery;* Blackmon, *Slavery by Another Name.*

53. Andrew Delbanco, *Melville: His World and Work* (New York: Alfred A. Knopf, 2005), ch. 6; Davis, "Expanding the Republic," p. 584; John Stauffer, "Melville, Slavery, and the American Dilemma," in *A Companion to Herman Melville,* ed. Wyn Kelley (New York: Blackwell Publishing, 2006), p. 224.

54. The two most persuasive scenarios I have found for ending slavery peacefully are from Gary Nash and David Davis. Both focus on the Revolutionary era. Davis wonders "what the United States might have been like" if Georgia and South Carolina—the two most pro-slavery colonies—had remained loyal to the British empire during the Revolution and joined Britain's other Caribbean colonies. "This would surely have deepened the difficulties for British abolitionists but might possibly have saved the United States from a Civil War." Nash speculates that had the framers not allowed compromises to slavery at the Constitutional Convention, which appeased South Carolina and Georgia delegates, the institution might have been abolished peacefully and constitutionally by 1860. See Davis, *Inhuman Bondage,* p. 155; Nash, *Race and Revolution,* pp. 25–56, 151–158.

In another superb counterfactual rumination, Gary Kornblith argues that had Henry Clay been elected president in 1844 (rather than James K. Polk), the Mexican War would have been avoided and civil war indefinitely deferred, though he does not envision slavery being abolished in his scenario. See Gary J. Kornblith, "Rethinking the Coming of the Civil War: A Counterfactual Exercise," *Journal of American History* 90:1 (June 2003): 76–105.

3. Did the Abolitionists Cause the Civil War?

1. For a deeper explication of some of the themes in this response, see Manisha Sinha, *To Live and Die in the Slave's Cause: Abolition and the Origins of America's Interracial Democracy* (New Haven, CT, forthcoming).

2. Lacy K. Ford Jr., *Deliver Us from Evil: The Slavery Question in the Old South* (New York, 2009), p. 282; Tony Horwitz, "The 9/11 of 1859," *New York Times,* December 2, 2009.

3. Stephen Douglas quoted by Andrew Delbanco, Chapter 1 in this book; David Donald, "Toward a Reconsideration of Abolitionists," in *Lincoln Reconsidered: Essays on the Civil War Era* (New York, 1947), pp. 19–36; Clifford S. Griffin, *Their Brothers' Keepers: Moral Stewardship in the United States, 1800–1865* (New

Brunswick, NJ, 1960); David D. Hall, "Peace, Love and Puritanism," *New York Times,* November 23, 2010.

4. See, for example, George Fort Milton, *The Eve of Conflict: Stephen A. Douglas and the Needless War* (Boston, 1934); J. G. Randall, *The Civil War and Reconstruction* (Boston, 1937); Avery O. Craven, *The Repressible Conflict, 1830–1861* (Baton Rouge, LA, 1939).

5. Rayford W. Logan, *The Betrayal of the Negro: From Rutherford B. Hayes to Woodrow Wilson* (New York, 1965); David W. Blight, *Race and Reunion: The Civil War in American Memory* (Cambridge, MA, 2001); W. E. B. Du Bois, *Black Reconstruction in America: An Essay toward a History of the Part Which Black Folk Played in the Attempt to Reconstruct Democracy in America, 1860–1885* (New York, 1935).

6. Martin Duberman, *The Antislavery Vanguard: New Essays on the Abolitionists* (Princeton, NJ, 1965); Stanley Elkins, *Slavery: A Problem in American Institutional and Intellectual Life* (Chicago, 1959), parts 2 and 4; Thomas Bender, ed., *The Antislavery Debate: Capitalism and Abolitionism as a Problem in Historical Interpretation* (Berkeley, CA, 1992).

7. Manisha Sinha, *The Counterrevolution of Slavery: Politics and Ideology in Antebellum South Carolina* (Chapel Hill, NC, 2000) and "Eugene D. Genovese: The Mind of a Marxist Conservative," *Radical History Review* 88 (Winter 2004): 4–29.

8. Drew Gilpin Faust, *James Henry Hammond and the Old South: A Design for Mastery* (Baton Rouge, LA, 1982); James W. C. Pennington, *The Fugitive Blacksmith: or, Events in the History of James W. C. Pennington, Pastor of a Presbyterian Church, New York, Formerly a Slave in the State of Maryland, United States* (London, 1849), pp. iv–x.

9. David Brion Davis, *The Problem of Slavery in Western Culture* (Ithaca, NY, 1966) and *The Problem of Slavery in the Age of Revolution* (Ithaca, NY, 1975).

10. Gary B. Nash, *The Forgotten Fifth: African Americans in the Age of Revolution* (Cambridge, MA, 2006); Douglas R. Egerton, *Death or Liberty: African Americans and Revolutionary America* (New

York, 2009); James Sidbury, *Becoming African in America: Race and Nation in the Early Black Atlantic* (New York, 2007); Manisha Sinha, "An Alternative Tradition of Radicalism: African American Abolitionists and the Metaphor of Revolution, 1775–1865," in *Contested Democracy: Freedom, Race and Power in American History,* ed. Manisha Sinha and Penny Von Eschen (New York, 2007); David Walker, *Walker's Appeal, in Four Articles, Together with a Preamble, to the Colored Citizens of the World, But in Particular, and Very Expressly to those of the United States of America. Written in Boston, September 28, 1829,* 2nd ed. with corrections (Boston, 1830), in *Walker's Appeal with a Brief Sketch of His Life By Henry Highland Garnet and Also Garnet's Address to the Slaves of the United States of America* (New York, 1848); James W. C. Pennington, *A Text Book of the Origin and History, &c. &c. of the Colored People* (Hartford, 1841).

11. David Waldstreicher, *Slavery's Constitution: From Revolution to Ratification* (New York, 2009); Leon F. Litwack, *North of Slavery: The Negro in the Free States, 1790–1860* (Chicago, 1961).

12. This argument has been made by Gary B. Nash, *Race and Revolution* (Madison, WI, 1980), and Paul Finkelman, *Slavery and the Founders: Race and Liberty in the Age of Jefferson* (New York, 1996).

13. Christopher Schmidt-Nowara, *Empire and Antislavery: Spain, Cuba, and Puerto Rico, 1833–1874* (Pittsburgh, 1999); Adam Rothman, *Slave Country: American Expansion and the Origins of the Deep South* (Cambridge, MA, 2005); Eugene D. Genovese, *"Slavery Ordained of God": The Southern Slaveholders' View of Biblical History and Modern Politics* (Gettysburg, PA, 1985); Daniel Raymond, Esq., *Thoughts on Political Economy* (Baltimore, 1820), p. 456.

14. Roy Basler, ed., *The Collected Works of Abraham Lincoln,* vol. 2 (New Brunswick, NJ, 1953).

15. George M. Fredrickson, *The Black Image in the White Mind: The Debate on Afro-American Character and Destiny, 1817–1914* (New York, 1971), chs. 1 and 4; Benjamin Quarles, *Black*

Abolitionists (New York, 1969); Paul Goodman, *Of One Blood: Abolitionism and the Origins of Racial Equality* (Berkeley, CA, 1998); Timothy Patrick McCarthy and John Stauffer, eds., *Prophets of Protest: Reconsidering the History of American Abolitionism* (New York, 2006); Manisha Sinha, "Black Abolitionism: The Assault on Southern Slavery and the Struggle for Racial Equality," in *Slavery in New York*, ed. Ira Berlin and Leslie Harris (New York, 2005), pp. 239–262.

16. Edward Bartlett Rugemer, *The Problem of Emancipation: The Caribbean Roots of the American Civil War* (Baton Rouge, LA, 2008).

17. James M. McPherson, *The Struggle for Equality: Abolitionists and the Negro in the Civil War and Reconstruction* (Princeton, NJ, 1964); Eric Foner, *Free Soil, Free Labor, Free Men: The Ideology of the Republican Party before the Civil War* (New York, 1970), pp. 74–75, 109–110.

18. Leonard L. Richards, *"Gentlemen of Property and Standing": Anti-Abolition Mobs in Jacksonian America* (New York, 1970) and *The Life and Times of Congressman John Quincy Adams* (New York, 1986).

19. I am grateful to Eric Foner for the information on Kennedy's changing views of Reconstruction.

20. Manisha Sinha, "The Caning of Charles Sumner: Slavery, Race and Ideology in the Age of the Civil War," *Journal of the Early Republic* 23 (Summer 2003): 233–262; David Donald, *Charles Sumner and the Rights of Man* (New York, 1970); Eric Foner, *Reconstruction, 1863–1877: America's Unfinished Revolution* (New York, 1988).

21. Eric Foner, *The Fiery Trial: Abraham Lincoln and American Slavery* (New York, 2010); Foner, ed., *Our Lincoln: New Perspectives on Lincoln and His World* (New York, 2008), part 2; John Stauffer, *Giants: The Parallel Lives of Frederick Douglass and Abraham Lincoln* (New York, 2008); James Oakes, *The Radical and the Republican: Frederick Douglass, Abraham Lincoln, and the Triumph of Antislavery Politics* (New York, 2007); David Donald, *Lincoln* (New York, 1995).

22. Aileen S. Kraditor, *Means and Ends in American Abolitionism: Garrison and His Critics on Strategy and Tactics, 1834–1850* (New York, 1969); Lewis Perry, *Radical Abolitionism: Anarchy and the Government of God in Antislavery Thought* (Ithaca, NY, 1973); Bertram Wyatt-Brown, *Lewis Tappan and the Evangelical War against Slavery* (Cleveland, 1969); Beth A. Salerno, *Sister Societies: Women's Antislavery Organizations in Antebellum America* (DeKalb, IL, 2005); Susan Zaeske, *Signatures of Citizenship: Petitioning, Antislavery, and Women's Political Identity* (Chapel Hill, NC, 2003); Julie Roy Jeffrey, *The Great Silent Army of Abolitionism: Ordinary Women in the Antislavery Movement* (Chapel Hill, NC, 1998); Patrick Rael, *Black Identity and Black Protest in the Antebellum North* (Chapel Hill, NC, 2001); John Stauffer, *The Black Hearts of Men: Radical Abolitionists and the Transformation of Race* (Cambridge, MA, 2001); Stanley Harrold, *Border War: Fighting over Slavery before the Civil War* (Chapel Hill, NC, 2010). For an overview, see James Brewer Stewart, *Holy Warriors: The Abolitionists and American Slavery* (New York, 1976).

23. *The Liberator,* January 2, 1836; Sean Wilentz, *The Rise of American Democracy: From Jefferson to Lincoln* (New York, 2005), pp. 422–425; Dwight Lowell Dumond, *Antislavery: The Crusade for Freedom in America* (Ann Arbor, MI, 1961); Foner, *Free Soil, Free Labor, Free Men;* Richard H. Sewell, *Ballots for Freedom: Antislavery Politics in the United States, 1837–1860* (New York, 1976); Frederick J. Blue, *No Taint of Compromise: Crusaders in Antislavery Politics* (Baton Rouge, LA, 2006); Bruce Laurie, *Beyond Garrison: Antislavery and Social Reform* (Cambridge, UK, 2005); Reinhard O. Johnson, *The Liberty Party, 1840–1848: Antislavery Third-Party Politics in the United States* (Baton Rouge, LA, 2009); James Brewer Stewart, *Abolitionist Politics and the Coming of the Civil War* (Amherst, MA, 2008).

24. Gilbert Hobbs Barnes, *The Antislavery Impulse, 1830–1844* (New York, 1933); Whitney R. Cross, *The Burned-Over District: The Social and Intellectual History of Enthusiastic Religion in*

Western New York, 1800–1850 (Ithaca, NY, 1950); Robert H. Abzug, *Passionate Liberator: Theodore Dwight Weld and the Dilemma of Reform* (New York, 1980) and *Cosmos Crumbling: American Reform and the Religious Imagination* (New York, 1994).

25. Ellen Carol DuBois, *Feminism and Suffrage: The Emergence of an Independent Women's Movement in America, 1848–1869* (Ithaca, NY, 1978); Eric Foner, "Abolitionism and the Labor Movement in Ante-bellum America," in *Politics and Ideology in the Age of the Civil War* (New York, 1980), ch. 4; R. J. M. Blackett, *Building an Antislavery Wall: Black Americans in the Atlantic Abolitionist Movement, 1830–1860* (Baton Rouge, LA, 1983); William Caleb McDaniel, "Our Country Is the World: Radical American Abolitionists Abroad" (PhD diss., Johns Hopkins University, 2006); Angela F. Murphy, *American Slavery, Irish Freedom: Abolition, Immigrant Citizenship, and the Transatlantic Movement for Irish Repeal* (Baton Rouge, LA, 2010); Mischa Honeck, *We Are the Revolutionists: German-Speaking Immigrants and American Abolitionists after 1848* (Athens, GA, 2011).

26. John R. McKivigan, *The War against Proslavery Religion: Abolitionism and the Northern Churches, 1830–1865* (Ithaca, NY, 1984); Charles C. Goen, *Broken Churches, Broken Nation: Denominational Schisms and the Coming of the American Civil War* (Macon, GA, 1985); Mark A. Noll, *The Civil War as a Theological Crisis* (Chapel Hill, NC, 2006); Harry S. Stout, *Upon the Altar of the Nation: A Moral History of the American Civil War* (New York, 2006); Genovese, *"Slavery Ordained of God."* For the 1995 Southern Baptist resolution see "Resolution on Racial Reconciliation on the 150th Anniversary of the Southern Baptist Convention," June 1995, http://www.sbc.net/resolutions/amResolution.asp?ID=899.

27. Eddi Glaude Jr., *Exodus! Religion, Race, and Nation in Early Nineteenth-Century Black America* (Chicago, 2000); Vincent Harding, *There Is a River: The Black Struggle for Freedom in America* (New York, 1981); Manisha Sinha, "His Truth Is

Marching On: John Brown and the Fight for Racial Justice," *Civil War History* 52 (June 2006): 161–169.

4. The Invisibility of Black Abolitionists

1. In addition to the works cited in the text and below, the following sources provided helpful background in the preparation of this essay: Ira Berlin, Marc Favreau, and Steven F. Miller, eds., *Remembering Slavery: African Americans Talk about Their Personal Experiences of Slavery and Emancipation* (New York: New Press, 1998); Christopher Alan Bracey, *Saviors or Sellouts: The Promise of Black Conservatives, from Booker T. Washington to Condoleezza Rice* (Boston: Beacon Press, 2008); Lawanda Cox, *Lincoln and Black Freedom: A Study in Presidential Leadership* (Columbia: University of South Carolina Press, 1981); Maurice S. Lee, *Slavery, Philosophy, and American Literature, 1830–1860* (New York: Cambridge University Press, 2005); and Henry Mayer, *All on Fire: William Lloyd Garrison and the Abolition of Slavery* (New York: St. Martin's Press, 1998).

2. James M. McPherson, *The Struggle for Equality: Abolitionists and the Negro in the Civil War and Reconstruction* (Princeton, NJ: Princeton University Press, 1964), pp. 431–432.

3. Benjamin Quarles, *Black Abolitionists* (New York: Oxford University Press, 1969), pp. vii–ix.

4. Ibid., p. 167.

5. Ibid., p. 235.

6. Benjamin Quarles, *Lincoln and the Negro* (New York: Oxford University Press, 1962), pp. 68–70.

7. Ibid., p. 83.

8. Ibid., p. 91.

9. W. E. B. Du Bois, *The Souls of Black Folk* (Chicago: A. C. McClurg, 1903), p. 18.

10. Richard Hofstadter, *The Paranoid Style in American Politics, and Other Essays* (Cambridge, MA: Harvard University Press, 1965), p. 9.

5. ABOLITION AS MASTER CONCEPT

1. A very intelligent treatment of this general subject, and a judicious assessment of the midcentury Americanist scholarship, is Neil Jumonville, *Henry Steele Commager: Midcentury Liberalism and the History of the Present* (Chapel Hill: University of North Carolina Press, 1999), particularly chapter 8, "The Character and Myth of Historians at Midcentury, 1937–1997," pp. 195–229.

2. Walter Russell Mead, "The Birth of the Blues," found at the Via Media blog, http://blogs.the-american-interest.com/wrm/2011/01/24/the-birth-of-the-blues/, accessed March 24, 2011.

3. Max Weber, "Politics as a Vocation," in *The Vocation Lectures* (Indianapolis: Hackett, 2004), especially pp. 81–94.

4. Allen Guelzo, *Lincoln's Emancipation Proclamation: The End of Slavery in America* (New York: Simon and Schuster, 2006).

5. William Lloyd Garrison, "To the Public," *The Liberator*, January 1, 1831, in William E. Cain, ed., *William Lloyd Garrison and the Fight against Slavery: Selections from* The Liberator (Boston: Bedford Books of St. Martin's Press, 1995), p. 72.

6. Roger Lundin, ed., *Invisible Conversations: Religion in the Literature of America* (Waco, TX: Baylor University Press, 2009); and his masterful *Emily Dickinson and the Art of Belief* (Grand Rapids, MI: Eerdmans, 2004).

7. Nathaniel Hawthorne, "Earth's Holocaust," in *Mosses from an Old Manse* (New York: Modern Library, 2003), p. 302.

8. Ray Kurzweil, *The Singularity Is Near: When Humans Transcend Biology* (New York: Penguin, 2006).

9. Herbert Butterfield, *The Whig Interpretation of History* (New York: W. W. Norton, 1965), pp. 46–47.

10. Roy P. Basler, ed., *The Collected Works of Abraham Lincoln,* vol. 7 (New Brunswick, NJ: Rutgers University Press, 1953), p. 283.

6. THE PRESENCE OF THE PAST

1. It should be noted, however, that Sinha and Stauffer do not agree with each other about who deserves the honorific name

"abolitionist": Stauffer uses it loosely enough to include eighteenth-century critics of slavery, both Northern and Southern, who, in his view, "worked together in their hopes to end slavery," while Sinha restricts it to "second phase" antislavery activists who had given up on all forms of gradualism and sectional accommodation.

2. Margaret MacMillan, *Dangerous Games: The Uses and Abuses of History* (New York: Modern Library, 2009), p. 127; Michael Kazin, "Good History and Good Citizens: Howard Zinn, Woodrow Wilson, and the Historian's Purpose," in David Feith, ed., *Teaching America: The Case for Civic Education* (New York: Rowman and Littlefield, 2011), p. 149.

3. Jane Grey Swisshelm, quoted in David Goldfield, *America Aflame: How the Civil War Created a Nation* (New York: Bloomsbury Press, 2011), p. 445.

4. Michael Kimmage, "The Life of the Mind," *New York Times Book Review,* November 6, 2011, p. 31.

5. Whitman, *Brooklyn Daily Times,* May 6, 1858, in *A House Divided: The Antebellum Slavery Debates in America, 1776–1865,* ed. Mason I. Lowance Jr. (Princeton, NJ: Princeton University Press, 2003), p. 201.

6. Adam Kirsch, "Lionel Trilling and Allen Ginsberg: Liberal Father, Radical Son," *Virginia Quarterly Review* 85:3 (Summer 2009): 199–206.

ABOUT THE AUTHORS

ANDREW DELBANCO is the Mendelson Family Chair of American Studies and Julian Clarence Levi Professor in the Humanities at Columbia University. His most recent books are *College: What It Was, Is, and Should Be* (2012) and *Melville: His World and Work* (2005), which won the Lionel Trilling Award and was a finalist for the *Los Angeles Times* Book Award in biography. Other books include *The Puritan Ordeal* (1989), *The Death of Satan* (1995), *Required Reading: Why Our American Classics Matter Now* (1997), and *The Real American Dream* (1999). Professor Delbanco writes widely on American literature and culture in the *New York Review of Books, New Republic,* and other journals.

WILFRED M. MCCLAY holds the SunTrust Bank Chair of Excellence in Humanities at the University of Tennessee at Chattanooga, where he is also Professor of History. His book *The Masterless: Self and Society in Modern America* (1994) won the Merle Curti Award of the Organization of American Historians, and among his other books are *The Student's Guide to U.S. History* (2001), the coedited volume *Religion Returns to the Public Square: Faith and Policy in America* (2003), and

Figures in the Carpet: Finding the Human Person in the American Past (2003). He has served since 2002 as a member of the National Council on the Humanities.

DARRYL PINCKNEY, a frequent contributor to the *New York Review of Books*, is the author of a novel, *High Cotton* (1993), and, in the Alain Locke Lecture Series, *Out There: Mavericks of Black Literature* (2002).

MANISHA SINHA is Professor of Afro-American Studies and History at the University of Massachusetts, Amherst. She is the author of *The Counterrevolution of Slavery* (2000), coeditor of the two-volume *African American Mosaic: A Documentary History from the African Slave Trade to the Twenty-First Century* (2004) and of *Contested Democracy: Freedom, Race and Power in American History* (2007), and author of numerous articles. Her forthcoming book is *To Live and Die in the Slave's Cause: Abolition and the Origins of America's Interracial Democracy*.

JOHN STAUFFER holds the Chair of the History of American Civilization and is Professor of English and African and African American Studies at Harvard University. In 2009 he was named a Walter Channing Cabot Fellow at Harvard. His books include *The Black Hearts of Men: Radical Abolitionists and the Transformation of Race* (2002) and *Giants: The Parallel Lives of Frederick Douglass and Abraham Lincoln* (2008), which both won numerous awards. His essays have appeared in *Time*, the *New York Times*, the *Wall Street Journal*, the *New Republic*, *Raritan*, and the *New York Sun*.

INDEX